Ellet Joseph Waggoner:
The Myth and the Man

Ellet Joseph Waggoner: The Myth and the Man

David P. McMahon

And the Editorial Staff of Verdict Publications

Verdict Publications
Post Office Box 1311
Fallbrook, California 92028
U.S.A.

ISBN 0-89890-001-8

Printed in the United States of America

Contents

1

Exploding the Myth

Ellet Joseph Waggoner (1855-1916) was one of the most illustrious individuals in second-generation Seventh-day Adventism. His name will always be associated with the historic twenty-seventh General Conference held in Minneapolis, Minnesota, from October 17 to November 4, 1888. Together with Alonzo T. Jones, Waggoner there spearheaded a revival of justification by faith which ignited vigorous controversy within the Adventist community.

Although the "crisis"[1] subsided after 1903, the question of 1888 has flared repeatedly. Numerous efforts have been made to dampen the issue. But each new book on 1888 has only added more fuel to the fire.[2]

---

1. "Crisis" is A. V. Olson's expression. See A. V. Olson, *Through Crisis to Victory: 1888-1901*.

2. Lewis H. Christian, *The Fruitage of Spiritual Gifts: The Influence and Guidance of Ellen G. White in the Advent Movement*; Arthur G. Daniells, *Christ Our Righteousness*; LeRoy E. Froom, *Movement of Destiny*; A. L. Hudson, ed., *A Warning and Its Reception*; Olson, *Crisis to Victory*; Norval F. Pease, *By Faith Alone*; Arthur W. Spalding, *Captains of the Host*.

The subject of 1888 has now returned to agitate the Adventist community. Conferences such as those at Palmdale[3] and Washington, D.C.,[4] highlight the fact that justification by faith is once again the great issue in the church. As a result, there is considerable interest in the central figures of the 1888 episode, and particularly in E. J. Waggoner.

Robert J. Wieland has recently collected nearly two hundred Ellen G. White statements which appear to endorse the message of Waggoner and Jones.[5] Perhaps her best-known statement is this:

> The Lord in His great mercy sent a most precious message to His people through Elders Waggoner and Jones. This message was to bring more prominently before the world the uplifted Saviour, the sacrifice for the sins of the whole world. It presented justification through faith in the Surety; it invited the people to receive the righteousness of Christ, which is made manifest in obedience to all the commandments of God. . . . This is the message that God commanded to be given to the world. It is the third angel's message, which is to

---

3. On April 23-30, 1976, a group of nineteen leaders and theologians met at Palmdale, California, for a conference on the meaning of the gospel of righteousness by faith. A joint statement from the conference appeared under the heading, "Christ Our Righteousness," in the *Review and Herald*, 27 May 1976, pp. 4-7. Some of the papers presented at the conference were published by Jack D. Walker as *Documents from the Palmdale Conference on Righteousness by Faith*. This publication includes Dr. Desmond Ford's paper, "Ellen G. White and Righteousness by Faith," prepared for possible presentation at Palmdale. But it was not, in fact, delivered there. Furthermore, Walker does not include any papers presented by the North American participants.

4. For a brief summary of the Righteousness by Faith Symposium, held in Washington, D.C., from August 6 to 11, 1978, see the resume by Gordon M. Hyde in *Ministry*, Oct. 1978, p. 13.

5. Robert J. Wieland, *An Introduction to the 1888 Message Itself*, pp. 111-26. In 1950 two missionaries, R. J. Wieland and D. K. Short, presented a manuscript entitled *1888 Re-examined* to the General Conference of the Seventh-day Adventist Church. They asserted that the church had rejected the 1888 message and that there must be corporate repentance.

> be proclaimed with a loud voice, and attended with the outpouring of His Spirit in a large measure.[6]

The eschatological implications which Ellen G. White associated with the Minneapolis General Conference have heightened interest in Waggoner and the message of 1888. Adventism is an eschatological community. It has waited expectantly for the Holy Spirit in latter-rain power to "finish the work" and bring Christ's second advent. And it seeks to hasten His return by preaching "the third angel's message." Mrs. White's statements about the 1888 message are too emphatic to be misunderstood. She affirmed that the final events would have shortly ensued if that message had been accepted.[7]

The conviction has grown that there is no hope of finishing the work unless Adventism returns to 1888 and accepts what was there spurned by the majority of the church's representatives. This is why the Adventist

---

6. Ellen G. White, *Testimonies to Ministers and Gospel Workers*, pp. 91-2.

7. See the following statements by Ellen G. White:

"If those who claimed to have a living experience in the things of God had done their appointed work as the Lord ordained, the whole world would have been warned ere this, and the Lord Jesus would have come in power and great glory" (*Review and Herald*, 6 Oct. 1896; cited in Froom, *Movement of Destiny*, p. 581).

"Had the purpose of God been carried out by His people in giving the message of mercy to the world, Christ would have come to the earth, and the saints would ere this have received their welcome into the city of God" (*Australian Union Record*, 15 Oct. 1898; cited in Froom, *Movement of Destiny*, p. 582).

"If all who had labored unitedly in the work of 1844 had received the third angel's message and proclaimed it in the power of the Holy Spirit, the Lord would have wrought mightily with their efforts. A flood of light would have been shed upon the world. Years ago the inhabitants of the earth would have been warned, the closing work would have been completed, and Christ would have come for the redemption of His people" (Ellen G. White, *Testimonies for the Church*, 8:116; statement published in March, 1904).

"If every watchman on the walls of Zion had given the trumpet a certain sound, the world might ere this have heard the message of warning. But the work is years behind. While men have slept, Satan has stolen a march upon us" (idem, *Testimonies for the Church*, 9:29; statement appeared in 1909).

consciousness is obsessed with 1888.

During the 1950's Robert J. Wieland and Donald K. Short urged the Adventist leadership to make the special light of 1888 available to the church by reprinting some of the writings of Waggoner and Jones.[8] The leading brethren did not then respond to this suggestion.[9] Some of Waggoner's material, however, has recently been republished. Two titles were officially reissued in 1972.[10] Dr. John O. Ford has prepared and widely distributed a selection of Waggoner's writings.[11] Other works by Waggoner have also been made available through independent sources.[12]

---

8. "A re-print of both Jones' and Waggoner's studies on the subject of Christ's righteousness, as presented during the time when the Spirit of Prophecy recognized them as the Lord's special messengers, would be to this generation as streams of life-giving water in a weary desert. There need be no fear of extremism if their writings are utilized from 1888-1892, including a part of the 1893 General Conference Session studies. We believe that the world itself has never had the privilege of reading such clear teaching concerning the everlasting gospel as is presented in these buried sources" (Hudson, *Warning and Reception*, pp. 143-44).

9. For the Defense Literature Committee's comment on the suggestion by R. J. Wieland and D. K. Short for a republication of the works of E. J. Waggoner and A. T. Jones, see ibid., pp. 251-52. By 1975, however, a different position was taken. In February of that year, the Righteousness by Faith Committee, meeting in Takoma Park, Maryland, made the following resolution:

"Although a complete and adequate message of righteousness by faith is available in the Bible and the writings of Ellen G. White, . . . we recognize that the Lord sent Jones and Waggoner to call attention to certain truths that had been lost sight of or that had not previously been fully comprehended.

"Because we believe that a restudy of their distinctive emphasis would be helpful today, we suggest that our denominational publishing houses seriously consider republication of selected sermons, articles, and books that are relevant today and representative of the messages on righteousness by faith given during the 1888 era by Elders Jones and Waggoner" ("Righteousness-by-Faith Report," *Ministry*, Aug. 1976, p. 6).

10. E. J. Waggoner, *Christ Our Righteousness*; idem, *The Glad Tidings*, ed. and rev. Robert J. Wieland, 1972 ed.

11. John O. Ford, comp., *Lessons on Faith: A Selection of Articles and Sermons by A. T. Jones and E. J. Waggoner.*

12. Within the last two years, the Judgment Hour Publishing Company, 309 Chevallum Rd., Palmwoods, Queensland, Australia, has republished E. J. Waggoner's *The Gospel in Creation, The Glad Tidings* (unrevised) and *The Gospel in Galatians.*

In 1977 Wieland published a brochure entitled *An Introduction to the 1888 Message Itself.*[13] This book drew on the following Waggoner sources: *Signs of the Times* articles from 1889 to 1891, *Christ and His Righteousness* (1890), *The Gospel in Creation* (1894), Waggoner's articles in the British *Present Truth*, studies presented at the General Conference session of 1897, *The Everlasting Covenant* (1900) and *The Glad Tidings* (1900).[14]

Despite this resurgent interest in Waggoner, however, there has never been a thorough study of his works. Statements and claims made, even by men of stature, show that essential research has been neglected. Numerous myths about Waggoner have helped mold opinion for many present-generation Seventh-day Adventists. A reexamination of this field is urgently needed.

Waggoner's entire relationship to the revolutionary article of justification by faith is highly significant. If we are to properly judge the theological issues now confronting Adventism, we dare not ignore his contribution. It is therefore essential to know what he actually believed and taught. We must distinguish between the Waggoner of history and the Waggoner of Adventist mythology.

There is the myth that the message of justification by faith in 1888 was far more advanced than that taught by Luther or Wesley.[15] Wieland audaciously claims that the message of 1888 was "a preaching of 'righteousness by faith' more mature and developed, and more practical

---

13. This is a transcript of six sermons presented by Robert J. Wieland between 1971 and 1976.

14. Ibid., "Author's Foreword."

15. Kenneth H. Wood, "F. Y. I.—4" [For Your Information], *Review and Herald*, 18 Nov. 1976, p. 2.

than had been preached even by the Apostle Paul."[16]

Then there is the myth that Waggoner's writings *after* 1888 best represent his message at the historic Minneapolis conference.[17]

Despite Waggoner's personal moral aberration and defection from organized Adventism, there is the myth that he remained basically sound "in the faith."[18] We will present explicit evidence that Waggoner became lost in the fog of pantheism. Even those aware of his pantheism generally accept the myth that it did not develop until

---

16. Hudson, *Warning and Reception*, p. 50. The thesis that Paul preached only a "partial" gospel has been revived as recently as 1978. In the August, 1978, *Signs of the Times* the following declaration appeared under the heading, "Your Bible Says This About—The Three Angels' Messages": "Paul did not preach God's last-day message. . . . It is extremely unlikely that you will hear the message of Revelation 14 proclaimed, except in this magazine" (pp. 6-7). We should remember that the people at Galatia, Colosse and Corinth thought the same way. Of course, if the last-day message is to be beyond what Paul offered, we would not really expect that that message could be proved by the greatest New Testament writer. And if not by the greatest New Testament writer, then certainly not by the lesser ones. We believe, in contrast to the above statement, that God gave a full disclosure of the gospel to the apostle Paul. The faith which he delivered to the Romans, to the Thessalonians, to the Colossians and to the Corinthians was sufficient to equip them for life and to prepare them for death, judgment and the coming of Christ. The tragedy was that the early church did not really believe Paul gave them "the whole story." Wherein they looked at Paul's message as "mere," they had a passion for "more." They succeeded only in manufacturing another way, until the temple of truth became cluttered with human devisings and aberrations.

17. See Froom, *Movement of Destiny*, pp. 188-217; Hudson, *Warning and Reception*, pp. 143-44; Robert J. Wieland and Donald K. Short, *An Explicit Confession . . . Due the Church*, p. 33; Wieland, *Introduction to the 1888 Message*, "Author's Foreword."

18. *Seventh-day Adventist Encyclopedia*, art. "Waggoner, Ellet J.," p. 1385; Froom, *Movement of Destiny*, p. 530. It is interesting to note that the revised (1976) edition of the *Seventh-day Adventist Encyclopedia* omits the section, "He believed and advocated the fundamental SDA doctrines to the day of his death."

about 1900 or later.[19] We will show that pantheistic sentiments began appearing in Waggoner's writings in the early 1890's.

Further, there is the myth that the pantheistic sentiments in Waggoner's works have no intrinsic connection with his views on the human nature of Christ, the mystical atonement, the righteousness of God and "effective" justification. We believe that the historical record clearly demonstrates that Waggoner's pantheism was integral to his theological system.

There is also the myth that any of Waggoner's material can be identified with the message of 1888 merely because he was the author. But his theological thought gradually evolved. To ignore the difference between the early and late Waggoner is like failing to distinguish between the early and later teachings of Luther.

Finally, there is the myth that Waggoner's teachings enjoyed the full endorsement of Ellen G. White.

If Waggoner had merely historical interest, we might regard these myths with benign indulgence. But since his teachings have now been revived and thrust into prominence, we cannot treat this matter casually.

We believe Waggoner made a positive contribution to Adventist thinking. What he said in and around 1888 was the beginning of great light for Adventism. Ironically, many rejected Waggoner when he was basically sound and followed him when he became unsound. It is

---

19. Froom, *Movement of Destiny*, pp. 349, 355, 529-30. Even Robert Haddock, who deplores the scarcity of availability of source material dealing with the pantheism crisis and is critical of the lack of detail in the theological controversy over pantheism, places the surfacing of Waggoner's pantheistic sentiments too late (see Robert Haddock, "A History of the Doctrine of the Sanctuary in the Advent Movement: 1800-1905," p. 285). Others who have dated the commencement of Waggoner's pantheistic ideas around 1899 are Dores E. Robinson, *The Story of Our Health Message*, pp. 312 ff., and Christian, *Fruitage of Spiritual Gifts*, p. 280.

difficult to resist the thought that this strange turn of events may have been a divine judgment on that generation.

Employed as a denominational writer from 1883 to 1903, Waggoner was one of Adventism's most prolific authors. He wrote a number of books, numerous pamphlets and hundreds of journal articles. He dealt largely with topics related to the law of God and the gospel, including expositions of Isaiah, the Gospel of John and the Epistles to the Romans and Galatians. In undertaking our research, we have recovered nearly everything Waggoner published. We have also read virtually every major work on 1888.

Waggoner was at least partly the product of his times. He espoused ideas which had historical antecedents in theologians far more prominent than himself. That his developing pantheism coincided with similar theological developments outside Adventism emphasizes the need to explore possible external influences on his thought.

Dr. James Buchanan noted that "it would be difficult to invent a new heresy."[20] Some of Waggoner's views may have seemed startlingly new to members of the small and isolated Christian body to which he belonged. But anyone examining the history of theology can trace the record of those who previously held the same ideas. And they can observe the eventual consequences of those concepts.

In many respects Waggoner's history is lamentable. His star rose suddenly and shone but a few dazzling moments before plunging into pantheistic darkness. We do not dwell on Waggoner's aberrations with pleasure. But we believe they hold special lessons for our time.

---

20. James Buchanan, *The Doctrine of Justification: An Outline of Its History in the Church and of Its Exposition from Scripture*, p. 64.

Although this may well be the first thorough historical examination of Waggoner, we do not presume it will prove the last or the best. We freely admit that problems remain to be resolved. But we hope this effort will stimulate others to investigate this crucial phase of Adventist history. There is, for example, the tantalizing problem of Mrs. White's apparent change of position on the law in Galatians and her lost "testimony" to Joseph H. Waggoner.[21]

One of the impediments to objective research on E. J. Waggoner has been a superficial reliance on what Ellen G. White said about him. But to quote Mrs. White's endorsement of Waggoner is like quoting her endorsement of O. R. L. Crosier's article on the sanctuary.[22] Some have tried to use this endorsement to support everything Crosier wrote in the article. But careful investigation will show that Mrs. White took a number of positions decidedly contrary to Crosier. There is a great difference between full and qualified endorsement.

Admittedly, this raises questions on Ellen G. White's relationship to Waggoner. If he began to seriously depart from the faith after 1891, why did not Mrs. White issue a warning much earlier? Some refuse to believe Waggoner was enmeshed in serious error during the 1890's solely because Mrs. White continued to hold him in high esteem.

How could Mrs. White urge Waggoner to accept a

---

21. See Ellen G. White, Letter 37, 1887, dated February 18, 1887, written to E. J. Waggoner and A. T. Jones from Basel, Switzerland. Mrs. White's changed opinion regarding the law in Galatians can be noted in Ellen G. White, *Selected Messages*, 1:234-35.

22. Ellen G. White, in *A Word to the "Little Flock,"* p. 12. O. R. L. Crosier (1820-1913), a Millerite lay preacher and editor of *Day-Dawn* (Canandaigua, N.Y.), began an intensive and extended study of the sanctuary question after the disappointment of October 22, 1844.

Bible-teaching position at Emmanuel Missionary College (1903) when he had been teaching pantheistic sentiments for nearly a decade? This is a problem for Ellen G. White scholars. Rather than closing our eyes to Waggoner's teaching, we suggest possible explanations for Mrs. White's protracted silence over his errors. Perhaps she was impressed that the Lord did not want a confrontation until the issue had fully developed. Maybe she earnestly hoped Waggoner would regain his former soundness. Perhaps she knew that many of Waggoner's critics were only waiting to chortle, "I told you so,"and therefore said nothing. Maybe she did not know or, dare we suggest, was mistaken on some things—unless we wish to contend for her personal infallibility. Perhaps, most seriously of all, allowing even leading brethren to follow Waggoner was evidence of divine wrath upon those who had spurned the gracious invitation of 1888. Thus various possibilities could illuminate Mrs. White's relation to Waggoner. But her endorsements refer to the 1888 period anyway. It is not our purpose to explain Ellen G. White's statements here. We intend to use the primary sources in presenting what Waggoner actually taught.

In executing this task, we will follow Waggoner's theological development chronologically. His theological pilgrimage apparently occurred in three stages. First, there was the early Waggoner, who blazed into denominational prominence from the time he began working at the *Signs of the Times* around 1883 until he reached the zenith of his distinction at the Minneapolis conference of 1888. Next, there was Waggoner in transition from 1889 to 1891. In this brief period a vital shift of emphasis took place in his thinking. Finally, there was Waggoner's awful descent into pantheism after going to England in 1892 to become editor of the British *Present Truth*. There is no evidence he ever regained his former soundness.

We do not say this to deprecate Waggoner's character. His humility and graciousness were impressive to the end. He was deceived on some things. But he appeared transparently honest in his beliefs. He confessed Christ in spite of his confusion. His last plea seemed to have the spirit of him who cried, "God be merciful to me a sinner." And if indeed, as we fondly believe, this was Waggoner's final confession, then his life was not in vain—not because his life was justified by what he did or did not do, but because it was justified by that Infinite Love who, before Waggoner was born, rewrote his history in the holy history of Jesus Christ.

Justification by grace does not mean damnation to those with any sinful theology. If that were true, no one could be saved. As Robert MacAfee Brown reviewed the history of the church, he ventured to say:

> There must therefore be a place within the church for "dangerous" ideas. This is the risk Protestantism must run in the name of devotion to the truth it is always stultifying. The compensating weight of heresy may be necessary from time to time to keep the listing ship of orthodoxy from foundering. If so, we can hazard the guess that God has a special kind of affection for heretics, and even that he raises them up to fulfill his purposes when his usual means have been hampered by human self-sufficiency.[23]

If this be so, then God must have a special love for Ellet Joseph Waggoner. He used him to stir the Seventh-day Adventist Church in 1888. And He is using him for the same purpose today.

---

23. Robert McAfee Brown, *The Spirit of Protestantism*, p. 128.

2

A Biographical Sketch

Our central concern is an analysis of E. J. Waggoner's evolving theology. Yet that theology developed in a historical context. It will therefore be helpful to outline his career before following the course of his emerging ideas.

Born on January 12, 1855, Ellet Joseph Waggoner was the sixth child of Joseph Harvey and Maryetta Hall Waggoner. His father had joined the Adventist cause in 1852. Soon thereafter he became a leading Seventh-day Adventist preacher and writer, and remained active until his death in 1889.

Ellet J. Waggoner attended Battle Creek College and later graduated as a physician from Bellevue Medical College in New York City. For some time he served on the staff of Battle Creek Sanitarium. About this time he married Jessie Fremont Moser, whom he had met at Battle Creek College. We do not have a detailed record of these early years in Waggoner's career. But we do know that he and his wife moved to California about 1880.

In October, 1882, Dr. Waggoner had a remarkable experience while attending a camp meeting at Healdsburg,

California. Here is his personal account:

> Many years ago, the writer sat in a tent one dismal, rainy afternoon, where a servant of the Lord was presenting the Gospel of His grace; not a word of the text or texts used, nor of what was said by the speaker, has remained with me, and I have never been conscious of having heard a word; but, in the midst of the discourse an experience came to me that was the turning point in my life. Suddenly a light shone about me, and the tent seemed illumined, as though the sun were shining; I saw Christ crucified for me, and to me was revealed for the first time in my life the fact that God loved *me*, and that Christ gave Himself for me personally. It was all for me. If I could describe my feelings, they would not be understood by those who have not had a similar experience, and to such no explanation is necessary.
>
> I believed that the Bible is the word of God, penned by holy men who wrote as they were moved by the Holy Ghost, and I knew that this light that came to me was a revelation direct from heaven; therefore I knew that in the Bible I should find the message of God's love for individual sinners, and I resolved that the rest of my life should be devoted to finding it there, and making it plain to others. The light that shone upon me that day from the cross of Christ, has been my guide in all my Bible study; wherever I have turned in the Sacred Book, I have found Christ set forth as the power of God, to the salvation of individuals, and I have never found anything else.[1]

When Waggoner died in 1916, his friends found a letter which he had written to his old friend, M. C. Wilcox. In this letter he repeated the account of his remarkable experience in 1882.[2] Apparently it was a profoundly important event in Waggoner's life. It stimulated his deep

---

1. E. J. Waggoner, *The Everlasting Covenant*, p. v.

2. E. J. Waggoner, *A "Confession of Faith,"* pp. 5-6. Found on Waggoner's desk after his sudden death on May 28, 1916, this confession of faith was published posthumously by friends.

interest in the subject of justification by faith, on which he wrote and preached incessantly for many years.

In 1883 Waggoner was called to assist his father in editing the *Signs of the Times.* He met Alonzo Trevier Jones in 1884. They became lifelong friends and shared a passion for justification by faith. In other ways the two men seemed quite different. Jones was tall, awkward, abrupt, aggressive, and a self-taught man who had served in the United States army. Waggoner was short, articulate and much more irenic in temperament.

This same year Waggoner began to manifest his talents as a writer. The *Signs of the Times* carried numerous articles from his pen during the five crucial years preceding the historic Minneapolis conference of 1888. It was at this conference that he presented the lectures on justification by faith which had such profound repercussions on the young church.

The next year Waggoner traveled widely with A. T. Jones and Ellen G. White. They were united in an effort to revive the church with the message of righteousness by faith. From November 5, 1889, to March 25, 1890, Waggoner participated in a Bible school for ministers at Battle Creek. This school was repeated the following year. During this time he was located at Battle Creek and employed by the General Conference. The *Signs of the Times* meanwhile continued to publish his articles. At the General Conference of 1891 held at Battle Creek, Waggoner presented sixteen studies on the book of Romans.

In 1892 the General Conference appointed Waggoner editor of the British *Present Truth*, and he lived in England from 1892 to 1903. During those years he returned to the United States for the General Conference meetings of 1897, 1899, 1901 and 1903. He was a principal speaker at the Bible study sessions for all but the last of these conferences.

Between 1903 and 1904 Waggoner served as Bible teacher on the faculty of Emmanuel Missionary College, Berrien Springs, Michigan. Here he proposed that the Bible should be the only textbook used in teaching history, language, natural science, physiology, chemistry and astronomy.[3] The administration, however, had broader views of the students' educational needs. So Waggoner's rather bizarre approach to education was never implemented. At the end of the summer term in 1904 he left the college and went to Battle Creek to become co-editor of the magazine, *Medical Missionary*, with G. C. Tenney.

While in England Waggoner had become friendly with a Miss Edith Adams. Shortly after he returned from England, she arrived in Battle Creek as a patient at the sanitarium. Her recovery was rapid, and Waggoner soon arranged for her employment as a nurse in the Battle Creek Sanitarium. Later he arranged her appointment to the editorial staff of the *Review and Herald*. In 1905 Mrs. Waggoner divorced her husband on the ground of adultery. The next year Dr. Waggoner and Miss Adams were married. This terminated his membership with the church.

For several years before the breakup of Waggoner's marriage, he had been advocating "spiritual affinity." His view was that one not rightfully a marriage partner here might be one in the life to come and that this allowed for a present spiritual union. Mrs. White called these views "dangerous, misleading fables" similar to the fanaticism she encountered after 1844. She also said Waggoner had been sowing the seeds of these Satanic

3. Emmett K. Vande Vere, *The Wisdom Seekers*, p. 114.

theories in England "for a long time."[4] These remarks cast a cloud over Waggoner's ministry in England.[5]

After several years in Europe with his new wife, Waggoner returned to the United States in 1910 and spent his final years in Battle Creek. He worked in the laboratory of the Battle Creek Sanitarium, acted as chaplain and taught in the Sabbath School.

On May 28, 1916, Dr. Waggoner died suddenly of heart disease at the age of sixty-one. Elders A. T. Jones and G. C. Tenney presided at his funeral service, conducted in the Battle Creek Tabernacle. Waggoner's old friend, A. T. Jones, delivered the funeral sermon.[6]

---

4. Ellen G. White, Letter 121, 1906; cited in A. V. Olson, *Through Crisis to Victory: 1888-1901*, p. 313.

5. E. J. Waggoner was prostrated with "brain fever" in December, 1885, while serving as his father's assistant at the *Signs of the Times* office in Oakland, California. He was hospitalized at the St. Helena Rural Health Retreat until early February, 1886. In a biographical sketch of her father's life, Pearl Waggoner Howard records another critical episode of "brain fever" during the period of his ministry in England. She stated that "Many prayers went up, and the Lord answered." One wonders, however, whether residual complications of Waggoner's illness contributed to his later theological and personal aberrations.

6. The proceedings have been preserved in the November, 1916, issue of the *Gathering Call*.

3

The Early Waggoner: 1884

In 1884 the Advent movement was still an infant church with less than 30,000 members. The basic beliefs of Adventism, however, had been established. And Adventists had begun emphasizing their distinctive "truths"—such as Sabbathkeeping, the state of the dead and the investigative judgment—in a way that subordinated the eternal verities of "the common faith." In fact, many early Adventists were Arian in their Christology, and they were not fully settled on the person and work of the Holy Spirit.[1] In theological matters the pioneers were obviously immature. They majored on prophecy and eschatology. Above all, they emphasized the keeping of the law.

---

1. See esp. LeRoy E. Froom, *Movement of Destiny*, pp. 148-87. Cf. Erwin R. Gane, "The Arian or Anti-Trinitarian Views Presented in Seventh-day Adventist Literature and the Ellen G. White Answer."

Such recognized authors as Norval F. Pease,[2] Arthur W. Spalding,[3] A. V. Olson[4] and LeRoy E. Froom,[5] together with other prominent Adventist writers, have adequately recorded the church's arid legalism in the pre-1888 period. Norval Pease notes that "the masthead of the *Review* from August 15 to December 19, 1854, listed the 'Leading Doctrines Taught by the *Review*.' This list included absolutely no mention of justification, righteousness, or any related topic."[6] Looking back on the period, Mrs. White herself said that the "doctrine of justification by faith [had] been lost sight of"[7] and the churches were "dying for the want of teaching on the subject of righteousness by faith in Christ, and on kindred truths."[8]

When we say the Adventist community placed great stress on the law of God, we mean "the third use of the law." In theology this is the law as a rule of life for Christians. And there is nothing wrong with this emphasis. It is true to the Bible and the Protestant heritage and is in harmony with all the great Confessions of the Reformation churches.

The early Adventists also taught that perfect keeping of the Ten Commandment law is the condition of eternal

---

2. Norval F. Pease, "Justification and Righteousness by Faith in the Seventh-day Adventist Church before 1900."

3. Arthur W. Spalding, *Captains of the Host.*

4. A. V. Olson, *Through Crisis to Victory: 1888-1901.*

5. Froom, *Movement of Destiny.*

6. Pease, "Justification and Righteousness by Faith," p. 31.

7. Ellen G. White, "Camp-meeting at Williamsport, Pa.," *Review and Herald*, 13 Aug. 1889, p. 514. Cf. Mrs. White's comment regarding the situation in the time of John Wesley: "The great doctrine of justification by faith, so clearly taught by Luther, had been almost wholly lost sight of; and the Romish principle of trusting to good works for salvation, had taken its place" (Ellen G. White, *The Great Controversy*, p. 253).

8. Ellen G. White, *Gospel Workers*, p. 301.

life. Uninformed Campbellites may have debated this with the Adventists. Other adherents of a degenerate Protestantism may have denied this too. But the great Reformers of the sixteenth century, like Luther, Calvin and Chemnitz, recognized that God requires a perfect righteousness for salvation. The best Protestant teachers of the nineteenth century, like Thomas Chalmers, James Buchanan, Charles Hodge and Charles Spurgeon, also believed that perfect obedience to the law of God is the condition of eternal life.[9]

But there was a difference between early Adventist preaching and good Protestant preaching. Adventists generally taught that the Lord forgives past sins and then helps the believer keep the law as a condition of eternal life. On the other hand, the apostles, Reformers and sound Protestant scholars taught that under the covenant of grace Christ kept the law for us and thereby fulfilled the conditions upon which God gives eternal life to believers. Believing sinners, justified by Christ's imputed righteousness, will keep the law. But they will never keep it in this life to the satisfaction of divine justice. Their good works testify to their genuine faith in Jesus Christ. But this obedience to the law is not the basis on which God grants eternal life.

In general, the pre-1888 Adventist community thought differently. Of course, they would have acknowledged salvation by grace. But "saving grace" was understood as "assisting grace." It was to help the struggling believer keep the law well enough to stand in the judgment and be granted eternal life at last. No wonder poor souls in the church groaned under the burden of trying

---

9. In the previous century John Wesley had unfortunately defected from this orthodox Protestant position. Like the Neo-Nomians and most Arminians, he said that Christ brought in easier (evangelical) conditions such as repentance and faith.

to fulfill the conditions necessary for salvation! No wonder this fearful quaking at the foot of Sinai prepared them for a more excellent way! E. J. Waggoner was one of God's trail blazers in that era.

In 1884 Waggoner was an assistant editor of the *Signs of the Times* under his father, J. H. Waggoner. That year young Waggoner wrote ten significant articles on the law and the gospel. Considering his denominational background, we should not be disappointed that his early articles were somewhat immature and faulty.

Before beginning his own series, Waggoner reprinted an article by Rev. Philip S. Moxom from the Presbyterian periodical, the *New York Independent*. It was entitled "Christ 'the End of the Law.'"[10] Moxom showed that the "end of the law" (Rom. 10:4) does not mean the abrogation of the law but its perfect realization and fulfillment in Christ. Christ was the embodiment of the righteousness of the law.

Understandably, such comments would be well received by Seventh-day Adventists. But Moxom did not correctly state the way of salvation. He did not say believers are saved unto life eternal because the Mediator satisfied the claims of the law on their behalf. Nor did he say this perfect righteousness becomes theirs by God's gracious imputation. In fact, the writer seemed to deny the gospel of salvation by substitution, representation and imputation. Moxom concluded his article by asserting that men are saved by the infusion of righteousness into them. He said:

> Righteousness is not to be found in scrupulous, ascetic practices—a kind of moral gymnastics—but in Christlikeness. As that condition is progressively attained, the law

10. Philip S. Moxom, "Christ 'the End of the Law,'" *Signs of the Times*, 5 June 1884, pp. 338-39.

> passes into fulfillment within us. He who loves Christ loves righteousness, and so is transformed in his deepest impulses. He is assimilated to the character of him whom he loves.
>
> Christ is, then, the end of the law for righteousness; not the abrogation of the law, but its re-enactment in the sphere of the individual soul. . . .
>
> If he is ever to be saved—that is, if he is ever to be righteous—the law must pass within him, and become a free, internal impulse. Obedience must rise in the spontaneous choices of his heart.
>
> How can this be accomplished? Not by any compulsion, not by any fiction of imputed righteousness, not by any hard will-work and ascetic discipline, but by FAITH, by the acquaintance of the soul with God in Christ, by the sinner's coming into love with Christ through the revelation of Christ's grace and beauty, and by the ministry of that Spirit whom Christ unceasingly bestows.[11]

No one who is sound in the doctrine of grace will deny the need for the infusion of righteousness by the Holy Spirit. But this is for sanctification—the fruit of salvation. Believers are not saved by inward sanctification. Salvation by sanctification is only a refined doctrine of salvation by lawkeeping. Believers are saved *to* a life of sanctification, *to* the keeping of the law.

Moxom's aversion to the Pauline and true Protestant doctrine of salvation to life eternal by Christ's imputed righteousness may be significant. Waggoner showed evidence of a long struggle over the concept of imputed—forensic—righteousness until finally he rejected it altogether. One wonders whether Moxom sowed the first seeds of error in Waggoner's mind. Despite his defense of the binding claims of law, Moxom's article was contrary to the gospel.

---

11. Ibid.

In his first major work, published on June 19, 1884, Waggoner raised the question, "What are the conditions of eternal life?"[12] On the basis of our Lord's answer to the rich young ruler (Matt. 19:16-22), he argued that the condition of eternal life is perfect obedience to the Ten Commandments—perfect righteousness. In this, young Waggoner was sound.

The next week Waggoner wrote on the "Nature of the Law." This was an excellent statement on the greatness of God's law. The law is an expression of God's righteousness, a transcript of His character. "The better acquainted we become with God's law, the greater it appears to us. . . . It is so broad that it covers every act that any rational creature can perform, and every thought that the mind of man can conceive."[13]

On July 3 Waggoner discussed the subject, "Condemned and Justified." After showing that the perfect law of God condemns all men, he stated the way of justification.

> Christ was sinless; the law was in his heart. As the Son of God his life was worth more than those of all created beings, whether in Heaven or on earth. He saw the hopeless condition of the world, and came "to seek and to save that which was lost." Luke 19:10. To do this he took upon himself our nature. Heb. 2:16, 17; and on him was laid "the iniquity of us all." Isa. 53:6. In order to save us, he had to come where we were, or, in other words, he had to take the position of a lost sinner. Thus the apostle says: "For he hath made him to be sin for us, who knew no sin." 2 Cor. 5:21. It was this fact that caused him such anguish in the garden. He felt that the sins upon him were shut-

---

12. E. J. Waggoner, "An Important Question," *Signs of the Times*, 19 June 1884, pp. 377-78.

13. E. J. Waggoner, "Nature of the Law," *Signs of the Times*, 26 June 1884, p. 392.

ting him away from God. It was this that caused him, when hanging on the cross, to utter that cry of bitter agony, "My God, my God, why hast thou forsaken me?" It was not physical pain that crushed the life out of the Saviour of the world, but the load of sin which he bore. "The wages of sin is death." Rom. 6:23. Sin will cause the death of every one who is not freed from it, for "sin when it is finished, bringeth forth death." James 1:15. And because Christ was "numbered with the transgressors," he suffered the penalty of transgression.

But the suffering of Christ was not on his own account. "He did no sin, neither was guile found in his mouth." 1 Peter 2:22. He was one who could safely appeal to the law to justify him, for he had never violated it. The law had nothing against him. "But he was wounded for our transgressions, he was bruised for our iniquities." Isa. 53:5. He alone has done more than his duty—more than was required of him; consequently he has merit to impart to others. This grace is freely given to all who believe in him. Thus: Our past life has been nothing but sin, for whatever good we may have thought to do, it was far from perfect. But we believe implicitly in Christ, and have faith in the efficacy of his sacrifice; and because of this simple faith, Christ will take our load of sins upon himself, and we will be accounted as though we had never committed them. He can take them without fear of any evil consequences to himself, because he has already suffered the extreme penalty of the law for them. And since our sins are taken from us, we are as though we had never broken the law, and therefore it can have nothing against us—it cannot condemn us. So we stand before the court justified. Justified by what? By our works? No; justified by faith in Christ. Our works condemned us; Christ has justified us. And so Paul's conclusion is true, that "a man is justified by faith without the deeds of the law." Rom. 3:28.[14]

---

14. E. J. Waggoner, "Condemned and Justified," *Signs of the Times*, 3 July 1884, pp. 408-9.

This is the true biblical and Protestant doctrine of justification through the blood or penal sufferings—atonement—of Christ. Nevertheless, neither in this article nor in subsequent articles in 1884 did Waggoner have a doctrine of justification by the imputation of Christ's life of perfect obedience to the law. His doctrine of justification was therefore vitiated and fell short of a full justification to life eternal.

Since keeping the law is a condition of eternal life, or "full salvation" as Waggoner called it, on July 17 he showed how a justified believer will keep the law.[15] He cannot do it in his own strength. But God's grace will enable him to do it. Unfortunately, Waggoner had no concept of imputed righteousness. Justification for him was only forgiveness for past sins. With God's helping grace the believer must go on to fulfill the conditions upon which eternal life is finally granted.

With Waggoner, justification was not a full justification unto life eternal. It was the nonimputation of sin on the ground of Christ's passive obedience (death). To Waggoner, justification did not include imputation of righteousness on the ground of Christ's active obedience (life). Of course, if Christ did not fulfill the conditions upon which God grants eternal life, the believer must fulfill them. But while Waggoner's doctrine of justification was inadequate, he was nevertheless struggling with a great theme and making progress.

In his July 24 article on "Christ the End of the Law," Waggoner repeated the Wesleyan idea that justification is only for the sins of the past and that a justified

---

15. E. J. Waggoner, "A New Creature in Christ," *Signs of the Times*, 17 July 1884, pp. 424-25.

believer will keep the law by the assisting grace of God.[16]

On August 7 Waggoner discussed Romans 7.[17] He first dealt with "the second use of the law"—exposing sin and driving the sinner to Christ. This emphasis had been sadly lacking in most Adventist teaching. In his masterful *Commentary on Galatians*, Luther, of course, had hammered on the second use of the law and thus prepared for the powerful preaching of justification by faith.

Later in this same article Waggoner considered the man of Romans 7:14-25. He took the view that this man is an unconverted though convicted sinner. With God's help, he argued, "the law in its perfectness" can be "accomplished by us" because "I can do all things through Christ which strengtheneth me." This superficial perfectionism was prevalent in Waggoner's time. And it has strong adherents in the Adventist community today.

On August 28 Waggoner discussed the meaning of "under the law" (Rom. 6:14).[18] His articles continued under the same title for the remainder of the year. He argued that Paul's expression "under the law" simply means under condemnation of the law. Waggoner was obviously trying to champion the binding claims of the law. He gave no evidence that he ever broadened his view on the meaning of "under the law."

The Seventh-day Adventist Bible Commentary and scholars like Dr. Edward Heppenstall have shown that "under condemnation" does not adequately cover all that Paul means by "under law."[19] In Paul's expression

---

16. E. J. Waggoner, "Christ the End of the Law," *Signs of the Times*, 24 July 1884, p. 442.

17. E. J. Waggoner, "Christ the End of the Law" (concl.), *Signs of the Times*, 7 Aug. 1884, pp. 473-74.

18. E. J. Waggoner, "Under the Law," *Signs of the Times*, 28 Aug. 1884, p. 520.

19. *The Seventh-day Adventist Bible Commentary*, 6:541-42, 960.

to the Galatians, "Tell me, you that desire to be under the law," it does not make sense to substitute "Tell me, you that desire to be under condemnation." The Judaizers did not practice circumcision because they wanted to be condemned. They did it to be justified.

"Under law" sometimes means using the law as a *method* of salvation. This is legalism. As long as men think they must fulfill the law as a condition of eternal life, they are under the law. While it is true that a believer keeps the law, he does not keep it to fulfill the terms of God's covenant. That is the work of the Mediator. Apparently Waggoner did not grasp this aspect of justifying grace.

On September 11 Waggoner presented a summary. It reveals that he saw justification as a forensic act of God which deals with the sins of the past.

> 5. "Condemnation" is "the judicial act of declaring guilty and dooming to punishment."—*Webster.* It is the direct opposite of "justification," which is "a showing to be just or conformable to law, rectitude, or propriety." —*Ib.* Therefore since the law of God declares the whole world to be guilty before God, and will not justify a single individual, it follows that all the world are under the condemnation of the law of God. . . .
>
> 7. Since all have sinned, and come short of the glory of God, we are "justified freely by his grace through the redemption that is in Christ Jesus." Rom. 3:24. We are justified by faith alone, "without the deeds of the law." Rom. 3:28; for no amount of good deeds will atone for one sin. If a man had stolen a horse, abstaining from horse-stealing to all eternity would not in the least clear him from the guilt. If we are freed from past transgressions, it must be solely by an act of favor on the part of God.
>
> 8. This justification belongs only to those who believe in Jesus. Rom. 3:26. It is purely a matter of faith on the part of the sinner, and of favor on the part of God. Rom. 3:21, 22, 28. And therefore to obtain justification from past transgressions, the sinner has only to have sincere

faith in Christ. It takes just as long to be justified as it does to have faith in Christ, and no longer.[20]

Waggoner then answered those who used Galatians 3:24, 25 as an argument against lawkeeping. Departing from the accepted Adventist position that the law in Galatians 3 is simply the Jewish ritual law, he accepted the position of Adventist opponents that the law in Galatians 3, as in Romans 3 and 7, is especially the moral law. Waggoner met these opponents on their own ground and contended that the Ten Commandments are binding on all Christians.

These articles on the law in Galatians must have pleased E. J. Waggoner's father, Joseph H. Waggoner. Years before, Uriah Smith and James and Ellen White had opposed J. H. Waggoner's teaching that the law in Galatians was the moral law. But although silenced, he had never relinquished his position.[21] Now, in 1884, his son took up his cause on the law in Galatians with some advancement on his father's arguments. This gave Uriah Smith, the editor of the *Review and Herald*, and George Butler, the President of the General Conference, great distress. The controversy was to flare again in 1886.

In his concluding article on the law in Galatians, E. J. Waggoner showed that redemption is based on the historic atonement of Jesus Christ.

"Wherefore," the apostle continues, "in all things it behooved him to be made like unto his brethren, that he might be a merciful and faithful high priest in things pertaining to God, to make reconciliation for the sins of the

20. E. J. Waggoner, "Under the Law" (cont.), *Signs of the Times*, 11 Sept. 1884, pp. 553-54.

21. Smith to Ellen G. White, 17 Feb. 1890. Cf. Smith to W. A. McCutchen, 8 Aug. 1901.

people." Heb. 2:17. He was made "*in all* things" like those whom he came to redeem.

Some one may exclaim, "What! do you think that Christ was a sinner?" By no means, he was in all points tempted like as we are, *yet without sin*" (Heb. 4:15); he was absolutely good, the embodiment of goodness, yet he was counted as a sinner. In no other way could he be made "in all things" like his brethren, for they were sinners. In proof of this we quote 2 Cor. 5:21: "For he [God] hath made him to be sin for us, who knew no sin; that we might be made the righteousness of God in him." As a parallel to this, read Isa. 53:6: "All we like sheep have gone astray; we have turned every one to his own way; and the Lord hath laid on him [Christ] the iniquity of us all." He bore the sins of the world as though they were his own. If it were not so, he would not have died; for "the wages of sin is death." None can die except those in whom sin is found; our sins were laid on Christ, and accounted as his; and so, although personally "he knew no sin," he was made to suffer the penalty of the law as a transgressor. And herein is the unspeakable love of Christ, that the innocent should assume the crimes of the guilty, and die in his stead. It was because Christ had taken upon himself "the form of a servant," that he became obedient unto death. Some have thought it nothing less than blasphemy to speak of Christ, the sinless one, as being made a sinner, and suffering the penalty for sin, but it is from this very thing that he derives his highest glory. We simply state the fact as we find it in the Bible. This is the unfathomable mystery which angels desire to look into, and which will to all eternity call forth the love and adoration of the redeemed hosts.

We think a careful reading of the above, together with many Scripture texts for which we have not space, will convince all that to say that one is "under the law" is equivalent to saying that he is subject to its penalty as a sinner. Gal. 4:1-5, then, teaches the simple fact that in order to save those who, on account of having violated the law, were under the condemnation of death, Christ put himself in their place and suffered the penalty of the law. . . .

> Death is the curse which the law pronounces upon every transgressor; but from this Christ has delivered us (if we believe on him), by voluntarily becoming our substitute.[22]

This is not the mystical atonement that Waggoner later developed to the detriment of his entire theological thinking. Here he does not hesitate to describe the atonement in forensic categories. Christ was "counted" a sinner and suffered the judicial penalty of the law. Oh that Waggoner had always clung to the simple view of redemption by the substitutionary dying of Christ in history! The early and the late Waggoner clearly demonstrate that the simple, direct understanding of Bible truth is generally correct. Error, on the other hand, winds in a devious, mystical path like a crooked serpent.

On another point, Waggoner's explanation of 2 Corinthians 5:21—Christ was made sin for us—is undoubtedly correct and contrasts with his later teaching. This was not an "effective making" but a "judicial making." Although Christ was sinless, He was counted a sinner. The sins of men were imputed to Him. But subsequent controversy with Butler on the law in Galatians led Waggoner to argue that Christ was made sin by actually taking a human nature as sinful as the rest of mankind. In later years this became a prominent feature of his departure from all the forensic categories of biblical thought.

What advancement did the early Waggoner make over the Adventism of his time? Except for Waggoner's view on the law in Galatians, both Uriah Smith and George Butler made virtually identical statements on Christ's substitutionary death, justification for past sins and

---

22. E. J. Waggoner, "Under the Law" (concl.), *Signs of the Times*, 18 Sept. 1884, pp. 569-70.

enabling power for future obedience. Apparently both Smith and Butler were also aware that the moral law has a "second use" as well as a "third use." Did Waggoner then make any advance at all?

In our judgment he did. A message must be assessed by its emphasis as well as by its individual points of doctrine. The spirit in which a musical composition is performed is often more important than correct technical execution. With Waggoner, justification became a great preoccupation, a burning passion. He saw the greatness and grandeur of the law, which exposed the pretensions of all men and convinced all of their sinnerhood. This was just what Laodiceans needed—Laodiceans who boasted in their lawkeeping, confident that their lives could stand before the judgment of God.

4

The Early Waggoner: 1886

In 1886[1] E. J. Waggoner wrote thirty-three articles for the *Signs of the Times*. His theme was the relation of the law and the gospel. This theme was to bring a confrontation in the historic conference of 1888.

On January 21, 1886, Waggoner began with the law of God—its nature, its jurisdiction and its perpetuity. He stressed the great perfection, breadth and spirituality of God's law. The law enters into every area of human existence. It demands the utmost perfection not only in every word and deed, but in every secret thought and motive. In building a strong case for the claims of God's law, Waggoner referred to such men as John Wesley, Bishop Matthew Simpson and Dr. Thomas Chalmers. He made repeated and effective use of Romans 2:13: "The doers of the law shall be justified." If a man perfectly kept the perfect law, he would be justified. But no one of

1. Waggoner wrote very little in 1885. He was largely occupied with teaching at Healdsburg College and preaching at regional camp meetings.

this kind can be found. This was an excellent preparation for Waggoner's significant article of March 25 entitled "Justified by Faith." Here are the major points in this article.

First, Waggoner's definition of justification was forensic.

> *Justification* is "a showing to be just, or conformable to law, rectitude, or propriety." *Condemnation* is "the judicial act of declaring guilty, and dooming to punishment." The two words are directly opposite in meaning.[2]

Waggoner further demonstrated his understanding of forensic justification when he showed that it is remission for the sins of the past.

> By this process, the sins are taken away from the individual, so that he may be counted as though he had never committed them. . . .
>
> Christ takes upon himself the sins of all our past life, and in return lets his righteousness be counted as ours. When this is done for a man, the law can do no other than justify him. It demands perfect obedience in the life, and that is what it finds. It matters not to the law that the obedience which it finds in the man's life is not really his own; it is counted as his own; and since the obedience is perfect, the law cannot condemn. Christ suffered the penalty for the sins which the man actually committed (Isa. 53:6, 10; 2 Cor. 5:21; 1 Peter 2:24), and thus God can be perfectly just and at the same time may justify a man who has sinned. But this can be done only for those who have faith in Christ's blood.[3]

The expressions "counted as though," "counted as ours" and "counted as his own" clearly show that Wag-

---

2. E. J. Waggoner, "Justified by Faith," *Signs of the Times*, 25 Mar. 1886, p. 183.

3. Ibid.

goner saw justification solely in forensic terms.

Second, justification comes to man only on the basis of Christ's doing and dying for us. The death of Christ "made it possible for God to justify those who have faith in his blood."[4] Waggoner thus acknowledged that God could not forgive apart from the penal sufferings of Jesus Christ. In this, Waggoner was true to the Bible and to the best in the Protestant heritage.

Third, Waggoner showed definite development in his understanding of justification. He began to comprehend that Christ not only had to die to pay the penalty so there could be no imputation of sin. Christ also had to keep the law in His life so that His perfect obedience could be counted as ours. Waggoner saw that justification includes both the forgiveness of past sins and the imputation of perfect righteousness to the believer.

Fourth, Waggoner inconsistently maintained his view of justification for past sins only. This was apparently based at least partly on the unsatisfactory rendering of Romans 3:25 in the King James Version.[5] We appreciate

---

4. Ibid.

5. The expression, "remission of sins that are past" (KJV), fails to convey the true meaning of the text. Cf. the following more recent translations. Conybeare: "thereby to manifest the righteousness of God; because in His forbearance God had passed over the former sins of men in the times that are gone by." The New Testament in Basic English: "to make clear His righteousness when, in His pity, God let the sins of earlier times go without punishment." The Berkeley Version of the New Testament: "which was for vindication of His righteousness in forgiving the sins that previously were committed under God's forbearance." Revised Standard Version: "This was to show God's righteousness, because in His forbearance He had passed over former sins." Goodspeed: "This was to vindicate His own justice (for in His forbearance, God passed over men's former sins)." W. H. Griffith Thomas comments on this passage as follows:

"The immediate object of the manifestation of God's righteousness was its relation to sins overlooked up to that time. The world was thinking that God had permanently passed over and ignored human sin. Calvary was His answer, showing that He was not indifferent to it, but only taking His own

Waggoner's concern that justification not become a once-saved-always-saved indulgence for future sin. But he was not clear on the problem of inbred sin—original sin—which still cleaves to regenerate Christians. Even the obedience of regenerate saints falls short of the divine splendor of God's law. Although the Spirit lives in them and moves them toward perfection, they cannot stand before the law with their new obedience. A justification for past sins only, so long and so much a part of Adventist soteriology, is inadequate.

Last, Waggoner betrayed his inadequate concept of human sinfulness. He said, "The law of God is so extensive and perfect in its requirements that the best efforts of fallen man, unassisted, must fall far short of it."[6] That is true. And what Christian—Catholic or Protestant—would ever dispute it? But the scandal of the Reformation was its claim that because of inbred corruption, even the saints' best works in a state of grace fall short of the perfection required by the law. Waggoner did not have this insight. His inadequate doctrine of sin led him to propose that the believer could finally stand in the judgment and meet its standard through inward sanctification.

Although Waggoner presented the good news of justification at the beginning of the Christian life, his understanding was not fully Reformational and certainly not fully Pauline. Paul's message of justification is eschatological. He does not ask how a man can find a

---

time and way of manifesting His righteousness. The verse, therefore, teaches the utter impossibility of God overlooking human sin. . . .

"Thus, the Cross of Christ not only justifies men to God, but justifies God to men, for it cleared the divine character from all appearances of indifference to sin in the ages before Christ came" (W. H. Griffith Thomas, *St. Paul's Epistle to the Romans*, pp. 115-16).

6. Waggoner, "Justified by Faith," p. 183.

righteousness to start the Christian life in order to become sanctified enough to pass the judgment. Rather, he addresses the question, How can a man find a righteousness to stand in the final judgment?

On April 1 Waggoner discussed the relation between justification and sanctification. He appeared to make further advancement. He reemphasized both the purely forensic nature of justification and the doctrine of imputed righteousness.

> The law demands perfect and unvarying obedience, but it speaks to all the world and finds none righteous; all have violated it, and all are condemned by it. (Rom. 3:9-19.) Present or future obedience will not take away past transgression, therefore the law cannot help us. But Christ is perfect righteousness, for in him dwells "all the fullness of the Godhead bodily." Now God says that he will impute the righteousness of Christ to every one who will fully believe on him. Impute means, "to set to the account of." Therefore we are to understand that whenever we accept Christ, his righteousness is set to our account. Thus "the righteousness of God" is manifested in our past lives, even though we ourselves have never done a single act of righteousness. So we have the wonder of perfect obedience to the law, without a single righteous act on our part. The righteousness of God without the law—Christ's righteousness imputed to us. . . .
>
> Justification was simply the "showing to be just, or conformable to the law." His [a man's] justification was simply pardon for having violated the law; it was an act by which another's righteousness was put in place of his unrighteousness.[7]

After the believing sinner is justified, he begins to keep the law. This "continued obedience," said Waggoner, "is sanctification." It is "the work of a lifetime,

---

7. E. J. Waggoner, "Justification and Sanctification," *Signs of the Times*, 1 Apr. 1886, p. 199.

. . . not an instantaneous, but a progressive work."[8]

Waggoner seemed to hint at a justification not only for the past, but for the present sinfulness of the saints. He was not too explicit on this point. But he said:

> In our best efforts there is so much imperfection, that but for the continual imputation of Christ's righteousness to make up for our deficiencies, we should be lost. The best that we alone can do is bad. . . .
>
> The redeemed saint will have no cause for boasting over the lost sinner. True, the law, when applied to their lives, reports perfection in the one case, and only sin in the other; but the saint cannot boast, for without Christ he would have been nothing. If Christ had not put his own righteousness upon him, he would be in as hopeless a condition as the sinner.[9]

We wish we could be certain that Waggoner meant that the imperfection of our best efforts includes what the believer does under the impulse of the Spirit. But other statements made in 1886 lean toward perfectionism.

Any hope that Waggoner had recovered the true biblical and Protestant faith is frustrated by his article of April 8. He returned to his theme of 1884 that eternal life is given on condition of perfect obedience to the law of God. But again he failed to show that this condition is met by the obedience of our Surety and in the imputation of that obedience to the believer. Rather, he said:

> But life is promised to the obedient, and as Christ enables his people to obey the law, he thus secures to them eternal life. . . .
>
> To conclude, then, we have found that the design of the

---

8. Ibid.

9. Ibid.

> law was that it should give life because of obedience. All men have sinned, and been sentenced to death. But Christ took upon himself man's nature, and will impart of his own righteousness to those who accept his sacrifice, and finally, when they stand, through him, as doers of the law, he will fulfill to them its ultimate object, by crowning them with eternal life. And so we repeat, what we cannot too fully appreciate, that Christ is made unto us "wisdom, and righteousness, and sanctification, and redemption."[10]

Waggoner failed to link justification with the gift of eternal life. He failed to see that justification is eschatological, that eternal life is given in justification and becomes the believer's present possession. With Waggoner, eternal life was only a future hope. Eternal life is, of course, a future hope. But Waggoner failed to show that in faith the believer already possesses God's glorious future (Heb. 11:1).

On April 15 Waggoner reinforced his concept that we gain eternal life by keeping the law with God's help. "He [Christ] is the 'end of the law,' in that he enables sinners to keep it, and thus to secure the life to which the law was ordained."[11] How disappointing! Waggoner takes us to the very borders of the Promised Land and then turns us back into the old-covenant wilderness. But he was near the great breakthrough. In his *Signs* article of May 6 he could say, "Having accepted Christ, his righteousness is imputed to us, which makes us clear before the law."[12]

---

10. E. J. Waggoner, "Christ the End of the Law," *Signs of the Times*, 8 Apr. 1886, p. 215.

11. E. J. Waggoner, "Abolishing the Enmity," *Signs of the Times*, 15 Apr. 1886, p. 231.

12. E. J. Waggoner, "Under the Law," *Signs of the Times*, 6 May 1886, p. 263.

Why did Waggoner not link this perfect righteousness with a full justification to life eternal? He could not see that far. After glimpsing Canaan, he failed to grasp the full provisions of the covenant of grace. So he said, "And as sin brought condemnation and death, so, when we are cleared from sin and condemnation, continued obedience, or righteousness, brings eternal life through Christ."[13]

Waggoner's problem was partly that he never understood what Paul means by being "under the law." Paul does not simply mean "under condemnation" as Waggoner insisted. Paul means being under law as a *method* of gaining eternal life. A man who thinks eternal life is gained by his lawkeeping is "under law" or under the old covenant, even if that lawkeeping is by God's help. Waggoner could not fully break into the light of the new covenant.

Waggoner wanted to prove that the law must be kept by the justified believer. But in saying that the believer must keep the law in order to gain life, Waggoner again fell "under the law." If only he had understood New Testament justification! It is not just a matter of starting the Christian life. It is grasping the verdict of the final judgment in the now by faith. And then it is living in the joy and freedom of knowing we already have eternal life on the ground that Christ has kept the law for us. Keeping the law even with assisting grace does not secure what Christ's keeping of the law obtained for us. His obedience gained eternal life for us as a free gift. Our obedience testifies to our faith in Jesus and makes us colaborers with Him in blessing others.

On June 3 Waggoner proposed that the law is written

---

13. Ibid.

in the hearts of God's people after their sins have been forgiven. "That means that they will be enabled to keep it perfectly."[14] Waggoner apparently fell into the error, common to traditional Adventism, that in the old covenant a person attempts to secure eternal life by keeping the law in his own strength, while in the new covenant the believer secures eternal life by keeping the law in God's strength. But who is so uninformed as to say that eternal life is won by man's unaided efforts to keep the law? Certainly no sensible Roman Catholic scholar has ever said that. Even the Pharisee prayed, "God, I *thank Thee*, that I am not as other men."

Unfortunately, Waggoner could not see that all works fall short of the glory of the law. All works done before grace are blatant sin. And all works done after grace are still tainted with sinful human defilement—not because the Spirit's work is imperfect or impotent, but because the human channel is still a corrupt, fallen nature. No saint is ever without sin for a moment. He does not satisfy the law with his new obedience no matter how much he progresses in sanctification or how much he is filled with God's Spirit.

In the new covenant, God does not merely help us fulfill the terms of the old covenant. The new-covenant gospel is the message that Christ the Mediator has fulfilled the terms of the covenant between God and man. We may enjoy the benefits by being in Christ by faith. Those benefits are forgiveness of sins and the law in our hearts. But the law is not in our hearts so that we can take Christ's place in fulfilling the terms of the covenant!

---

14. E. J. Waggoner, "Under the Law" (concl.), *Signs of the Times*, 3 June 1886, pp. 326-27.

The Law in Galatians

On August 5 Waggoner began a series on Galatians 3:19-24. In his article of August 12 he reaffirmed justification by imputed righteousness and the need for being made morally perfect before the second coming of Christ.

> Christ imputes to the repentant sinner his own righteousness, which is the righteousness of God, and enables him to live up to the requirements of the law, thus making him "meet to be partakers of the inheritance of the saints in light."
>
> When Christ comes, this design will have been accomplished. Under the second covenant the law will have been written in the hearts (see Jer. 31:33) of all who have desired the better country, and thus they will "all be righteous," and fit to "inherit the land forever." Isa. 60:21. They will be righteous because the law is written in their hearts. They will then be as pure as was Adam when he was first created, with this advantage, that their characters will have been fully tested.[15]

On August 26 Waggoner used Galatians 3 and, significantly, Luther's argument in his *Commentary on Galatians* to emphasize the truth that the law is a schoolmaster to lead us to Christ.[16] Waggoner insisted that this second use of the law was the special office of the moral law. This emphasis was largely absent in Adventist writing and preaching.

Waggoner did not exclude the ritual law from Galatians 3. But the following week he cited John Wesley in

---

15. E. J. Waggoner, "Comments on Galatians 3," no. 6, *Signs of the Times*, 12 Aug. 1886, p. 486.

16. E. J. Waggoner, "Comments on Galatians 3," no. 8, *Signs of the Times*, 26 Aug. 1886, p. 518.

arguing that Galatians 3 is particularly concerned with the moral law.[17] On September 23 he used the writings of pioneer J. N. Andrews to affirm that the schoolmaster law refers to the moral law.[18]

In November Waggoner published an article by his father, J. H. Waggoner. The article clearly demonstrated that the father shared his son's passion for justification by faith. As E. J. Waggoner showed evidence of reflecting Luther, so J. H. Waggoner showed his indebtedness to the Reformation understanding of justification. J. H. Waggoner began by declaring:

> No apology could be in place for writing or speaking on the subject of justification by faith. Lying at the very foundation of Christian experience—the substratum of the work of the gospel on the human heart—it can never be dwelt upon too much. And when all has been said that human tongues can say, or that human minds can conceive, the whole truth on this great theme will not have been told.[19]

After stating that the "justification, or righteousness," "which is the subject of the apostle's argument in this letter to the Romans, is the treating of sinful man as though he were righteous," J. H. Waggoner quoted the great English Reformer, Richard Hooker.

> This . . . justification is, as is well stated by Hooker, "without us, which we have by imputation." This, again, is identical with the righteousness of faith; that is, we are

---

17. E. J. Waggoner, "Comments on Galatians 3," no. 9, *Signs of the Times*, 2 Sept. 1886, p. 534.

18. J. N. Andrews, "Christ and the Law," *Signs of the Times*, 23 Sept. 1886, p. 582.

19. J. H. Waggoner, "Justification by Faith," *Signs of the Times*, 25 Nov. 1886, p. 712.

> accounted righteous by reason of what some one does *for us*, and not by reason of our works or obedience.[20]

There is, however, a serious flaw in this article on justification by faith. Just as his son separated justification and eternal life—making one present and the other future, one attained by Christ's obedience and the other by ours—so Waggoner senior here distinguished justification and salvation, making the first present and the second future. In a subsequent article J. H. Waggoner said:

> Justification is not of or by works; . . . it places him [man] where he can work to divine acceptance. . . . Justification is for past sins, or for their remission; salvation is future, and is conditioned upon "patient continuance in well-doing." Rom. 2:7.[21]

The best exegetes acknowledge that justification and salvation are not identical terms. Salvation may refer to justification, to the process of sanctification or even to our deliverance at the coming of Christ. But we must carefully avoid the idea that justification falls short of bringing us salvation or that it is only a partial salvation. We receive a knowledge—an experimental possession—of salvation by the forgiveness of sins (Luke 1:77). Jesus declared, "Truly, truly, I say to you, he who hears My word and believes Him who sent Me, has eternal life; he does not come into judgment, but has passed from death to life" (John 5:24, RSV).

Justification is the verdict of the heavenly Judge that forgiveness is ours, heaven is ours, eternal life is ours,

---

20. Ibid. Would to God that E. J. Waggoner had stayed with this Reformation doctrine of a forensic justification by imputed righteousness alone!

21. J. H. Waggoner, "Justification and Salvation," *Signs of the Times*, 30 Dec. 1886, p. 792.

the inheritance is ours, the Holy Spirit is ours, a life of holiness is ours and everything Christ has is ours. In the verdict of the court we are given "all things." God pledges that He will make us holy and fit for heaven if only we "continue in the faith." Justification implicitly includes sanctification and glorification because it guarantees them. Justification therefore puts us in full possession of salvation. But we must understand that that salvation is possessed by faith.

We can sympathize with J. H. Waggoner's fear of antinomianism and a lazy once-saved-always-saved-ism. But he does not solve the problem by suggesting that justification is less than a justification unto the full salvation of life eternal.

If his son, E. J. Waggoner, also believed that justification was by faith alone but salvation was by lawkeeping, he certainly had not yet recovered either the Protestant or the New Testament faith. In the New Testament, justification, the gift of the Holy Spirit and salvation are all eschatological gifts. They are all ours by grace for Christ's sake through faith.

Controversy

Apparently Uriah Smith and George Butler had been following E. J. Waggoner's pen with considerable apprehension. To understand this we need to review some Seventh-day Adventist history.

In the formative years of Seventh-day Adventism, J. N. Andrews[22] and J. H. Waggoner[23] were foremost

---

22. J. N. Andrews, Reply to H. E. Carver, *Review and Herald*, 16 Sept. 1851, p. 29; idem, "Watchman, What of the Night?" ibid., 27 May 1852, pp. 14-15.

23. J. H. Waggoner, *The Law of God: An Examination of the Testimony of Both Testaments*, pp. 69-114.

among those who taught that the law in Galatians especially referred to the moral law. James White also believed that the law in Galatians principally referred to the moral law.[24] Looking back over those early years, George Butler observed that a majority of the leading brethren "accepted the view that the moral law was the main subject of Paul's consideration in the book of Galatians."[25]

In 1854 J. H. Waggoner published a pamphlet entitled *The Law of God: An Examination of the Testimony of Both Testaments*. He took the position that the law in Galatians was the moral law. But as the Sabbatarian Adventists became embroiled in controversy over the binding claims of the Ten Commandments, some believed they needed a stronger answer to Galatians 3:24, 25: "Wherefore the law was our schoolmaster to bring us unto Christ, that we might be justified by faith. But after that faith is come, we are no longer under a schoolmaster." They felt that if they took the position that this scripture referred to the ceremonial law, they could better answer the anti-Sabbatarians. Thus, in 1856 the brethren in Vermont became greatly concerned over the publication of Waggoner's pamphlet. They sent Stephen Pierce to Battle Creek to investigate J. H. Waggoner's position.

J. H. Waggoner refused to stay in Battle Creek for the examination, but returned to his home in Burlington.

---

24. James White, "Justified by the Law," *Review and Herald*, 10 June 1852, p. 24.

25. George I. Butler, *The Law in the Book of Galatians: Is It the Moral Law, or Does It Refer to that System of Laws Peculiarly Jewish?* p. 3. This work was issued to coincide with the commencement of the 1886 General Conference session on November 18.

Nevertheless, meetings were held with Elder Pierce at Battle Creek. Uriah Smith and James and Ellen White were present. For three days the whole question was thoroughly discussed. Apparently Pierce convincingly defended his proposition that the law in Galatians was the Mosaic law. J. H. Waggoner's view was repudiated. Smith records that "Sr. White shortly after this had a vision in which this law question was shown her, and she immediately wrote J. H. W. that his position on the law was wrong, and Bro. Pierce was right."[26]

As a result James White withdrew J. H. Waggoner's book from the market. Despite J. H. Waggoner's repeated solicitations to have his book republished, James White replied, "NOT until you revise your position on the law." Waggoner refused to do this, so the book was never reissued.[27] This provides a historical background for the controversy which ensued in 1886.

The Butler-Waggoner Exchange

In November, 1886, George Butler, the President of the General Conference, published an eighty-five page booklet entitled *The Law in the Book of Galatians: Is It the Moral Law, or Does It Refer to that System of Laws Peculiarly Jewish?* It was issued on the opening day of the 1886 General Conference, held at Battle Creek. This work did not mention E. J. Waggoner's name. But it was obviously intended as an official refutation of Waggoner's articles in the *Signs of the Times* on the law in

26. Smith to W. A. McCutchen, 8 Aug. 1901. Cf. Smith to White, 17 Feb. 1890.

27. Smith to McCutchen, 8 Aug. 1901.

Galatians. In his booklet Butler acknowledged that in the early years of the pioneer period the law in Galatians was thought to be the moral law. He went on to say:

> But there came quite a change in this respect at a later period, when some of our leading brethren, to whom our people have ever looked as safe counsellors in questions of perplexity, gave up the view that the moral law was mainly under discussion, and took the position that it was the ceremonial law. Many others who have come later to act a part in the work, have accepted the latter view with strong confidence.[28]

In his booklet Butler stated his reasons for believing that the law spoken of in Galatians refers to the ceremonial law, which passed away at the cross. Not satisfied with arguing his view, he expressed deep concern that the contrary position was being revived.

> The writer acknowledges considerable surprise that during the last year or two the subject has been made quite prominent in the instructions given to those at Healdsburg College preparing to labor in the cause; also in the lessons passing through the *Instructor*, designed for our Sabbath-schools all over the land, and in numerous argumentative articles in the *Signs of the Times*, our pioneer missionary paper, thus throwing these views largely before the reading public not acquainted with our faith. Thus, strong and repeated efforts have been made to sustain the view that the moral law is the subject of the apostle's discourse in the letter to the Galatians.[29]

Butler felt that ecclesiastical pressure was also needed to secure unity and to prevent Waggoner's view from be-

---

28. Butler, *Law in Galatians*, p. 3.
29. Ibid., p. 4.

ing agitated. He therefore brought the matter to the attention of the Theological Committee at the General Conference session of December 6. A resolution, designed to suppress the publication of views contrary to the position "held by a fair majority of our people" unless these views had first been "examined and approved by the leading brethren of experience," was passed.[30]

On February 10, 1887, Waggoner prepared a seventy-one page open letter to Butler called *The Gospel in the Book of Galatians: A Review*. His letter was largely a closely reasoned defense of his view that the law passages in Galatians refer to the moral law. We believe this represents some of his finest writing.

Although Waggoner presented the better argument, he overstated his case when he said that in Galatians 3:24, 25 "the reference must be to the moral law, and to that alone."[31] Moreover, Galatians 3:19 refers primarily to the historical coming of Christ with its dispensational changes as Butler claimed. And "under the law" does not always mean "under condemnation" as Waggoner insisted.[32]

Although Waggoner's answer to Butler contains no exposition of justification by faith, it reveals Waggoner's high estimate of this doctrine. Whereas Butler referred to it as "the much-vaunted doctrine of justification by faith,"[33] Waggoner retorted:

---

30. *The Seventh-day Adventist Year Book: 1887*, pp. 45-6. The members of this committee were George I. Butler, S. N. Haskell, D. M. Canright, E. J. Waggoner, J. H. Morrison, Uriah Smith, M. C. Wilcox, B. L. Whitney and Wm. Covert.

31. E. J. Waggoner, *The Gospel in the Book of Galatians: A Review*, p. 43. This letter was written on February 10, 1887.

32. Butler, *Law in Galatians*, p. 51.

33. Ibid., p. 78.

> Before I close, I cannot refrain from expressing my regret to see in your book (on page 78) the expression, "The much-vaunted doctrine of justification by faith." Do you know of any other means of justification? Your words seem to intimate that you think that doctrine has been overestimated. Of one thing I am certain, and that is, that those who have held to the theory of the law, which you are endeavoring to uphold, have not overestimated the doctrine of justification by faith; because that theory leads inevitably to the conclusion that men are justified by the law. But when I read Rom. 3:28, and read also that Paul knew nothing among the Corinthians but Jesus Christ and him crucified, and that "the just shall *live* by faith," and that "this is the victory that overcometh the world, even our faith" (1 John 5:4), and that Paul wanted to be found when Christ comes, having nothing but "the righteousness which is of God by faith" (Phil. 3:9), I conclude that it is *impossible to overestimate the doctrine of justification by faith.* You may call it a "much-*vaunted*" doctrine if you please; I accept the word, and say with Paul: "God forbid that I should glory [or vaunt], save in the cross of our Lord Jesus Christ, by whom the world is crucified unto me, and I unto the world."[34]

Waggoner not only revealed his great obsession with the doctrine of justification by faith. He also showed great respect for the Reformation of the sixteenth century. The clash between Butler and Waggoner was a classic conflict between ecclesiastical conservatism and the real spirit of Protestantism. Butler resisted change, because he feared anything which might reveal that the church had ever taught anything amiss. On the other hand, Waggoner felt the admission of past mistakes would be a sign of strength rather than weakness. Said Waggoner:

34. Waggoner, *Gospel in Galatians*, pp. 70-71.

> If our people should *to-day*, as a body (as they will sometime), change their view on this point, it would simply be an acknowledgment that they are better informed to-day than they were yesterday. It would simply be taking an advance step, which is never humiliating except to those whose pride of opinion will not allow them to admit that they can be wrong. It would simply be a step nearer the faith of the great Reformers from the days of Paul to the days of Luther and Wesley. It would be a step closer to the heart of the Third Angel's Message. I do not regard this view which I hold as a new idea at all. It is not a new theory of doctrine. Everything that I have taught is perfectly in harmony with the fundamental principles of truth which have been held not only by our people, but by all the eminent reformers. And so I do not take any credit to myself for advancing it. All I claim for the theory is, that it is consistent, because it sticks to the fundamental principles of the gospel.[35]

Waggoner, however, deferred publication of his reply to Butler until December, 1888, a month after the Minneapolis conference. This gives some evidence of Waggoner's conciliatory spirit. The real cause of the delay, however, may have been the letter he received from Mrs. White, dated February 18, 1887.

> If you, my brethren had the experience, that my husband and myself have had in regard to these known differences being published in articles in our papers, you never would have pursued the course you have, either in your ideas advanced before our students in college, neither would it have appeared in the "Signs." Especially at this time should everything like differences be repressed. . . . You must as far as differences are concerned be wise as serpents and harmless as doves. Even if you are fully convinced that your ideas of doctrine are sound, you do not show wisdom that that difference should be

35. Ibid., p. 70.

made apparent. I have no hesitancy in saying that you have made a mistake. You have departed from the positive directions God has given on this matter, and only harm will be the result. This is not in God's order. You have now set the example for others to do as you have done, to feel at liberty to put in their various ideas and theories and bring in a state of things you have not dreamed of. . . . It is no small matter for you to come out in the "Signs" as you have done, and God has plainly revealed that such things should not be done. We must keep before the world a united front. Satan will triumph to see differences among Seventh-day Adventists. These questions are not vital points. I have not read Elder Butler's pamphlet or any articles written by any of our writers and I do not mean to. . . . The matter does not lie clear and distinct in my mind yet. I cannot grasp the matter, and for this reason I am fully convinced that in the presenting it has not only been untimely, but deleterious. Elder Butler has had such an amount of burdens he was not prepared to do this subject justice. Brother E. J. Waggoner has had his mind exercised on this subject, but to bring differences into the General Conference is a mistake; it should not be done. There are those who do not go deep, who are not Bible students, who will take positions decidedly for or against, grasping at apparent evidence; yet it may not be truth, and to take differences into our conferences where the differences become widespread, and sending forth all through the field various ideas, one in opposition to the other, is not God's plan but at once raises questionings and doubts whether we have the truth whether after all we are not mistaken and in error.

The Reformation was greatly retarded by making prominent differences in some points of faith and each party holding tenaciously to those things where they differed. We shall see eye to eye ere long, but to become firm and consider it your duty to present your views in decided opposition to the faith or truth as it has been taught by us as a people, is a mistake, and will result in harm, and only harm, as in the days of Martin Luther. Beginning to draw apart and feel at liberty to express your ideas without reference to the views of your brethren, and a state of things will be introduced that you do not dream of. My husband had some ideas on some points different from the views taken by his brethren. I was shown however true his views were, God did not call for him to put them in front before his brethren and create differences of ideas. While he might hold these views subordinate himself, once made public and minds would seize, and just because others believed differently would make this difference the whole burden of the message, and get up contention and variance. There are the main pillars of our faith, subjects which are of vital interest, the Sabbath and keeping the commandments of God, and speculative ideas should not be agitated. For there are peculiar minds that love to get some point that others do not believe, and argue and attract attention to that one point, urge that point, magnify that point, when really it is a point which is not of vital importance and will be understood differently. Twice I have been shown that everything of a character to cause our brethren to be divided from the very points now essential for this time, should be kept in the background. Christ did not reveal many things that were true because it would create a difference of opinion and get up dissatisfaction, but young men who have not passed through the experience we have had would as soon have a brush as not. Nothing would suit them better than a sharp discussion. If these things come into our Conference, I would refuse to attend one of them; for I have so much light upon this subject that I know that unconsecrated and unsanctified hearts would enjoy this kind of exercise. Too late in the day, brethren, too late in the day. We are in the great day of atonement, a time when a man must be afflicting his soul, confessing his sins, humbling his heart before God, and getting ready for the conflict. When these contentions come in before the people they will think one has the argument, and that another decidedly opposed has the argument, the poor people become confused and the Conference will be a dead loss, worse than though they had no conference. Now when everything is in dissension and strife, there must be decided effort to handle, publish with pen and voice these things that will reveal only harmony. Elder Waggoner has loved discussion and contention. I fear that Elder E.

> J. Waggoner has cultivated a love for the same. We need now good humble religion. Elder E. J. W. needs humility, meekness, and Brother Jones can be a power for good if he will constantly cultivate practical godliness that he may teach this to the people. But how do you think I feel to see our two leading papers in contention? I know how these papers came into existence, I know what God has said about them, that they are one, that no variance should be seen in these two instrumentalities of God. They are one and they must remain one, breathing the same spirit, exercising the same work, to prepare a people to stand in the day of the Lord, one in faith and one in purpose.[36]

Mrs. White's letter to Waggoner and Jones, counseling silence, has often been partially quoted—especially by those wanting to avoid denominational controversy. But here we can learn an important lesson on using Ellen G. White counsels. Counsel is not absolute law to be invariably adopted. Circumstances can easily modify or even nullify the counsel.

A copy of Mrs. White's letter to Waggoner and Jones was sent to Butler and Smith. They took encouragement from it and, writing in the *Review and Herald*, attacked Waggoner's views on the law in Galatians. They also circulated Butler's booklet against Waggoner. Mrs. White protested this misuse of her counsel. Because of their attacks on Waggoner's position, she said it would be unfair to expect Waggoner to remain silent. Her letter is astonishingly frank. It shows how a new set of circumstances demands new counsel.

> Dear Brethren Butler and Smith:—
>
> I have sent copies of letters written to Brn. Waggoner

36. Ellen G. White, Letter 37, 1887. Copies of this letter were sent by Mrs. White to Butler and Smith.

and Jones to Eld. Butler in reference to introducing and keeping in the front and making prominent subjects on which there [are] differences of opinions. I sent this not that you should make them weapons to use against the brethren mentioned, but that the very same cautions and carefulness be exercised by you to preserve harmony as you would have these Brethren exercise. . . .

Now I do not wish the letter that I have sent to you should be used in a way that you will take it for granted that your ideas are all correct and Dr. Waggoner's and Elder Jones' are all wrong.

I was pained when I saw your article in the Review, and for the last half hour I have been reading the references preceding your pamphlet. Now my brother, things that you have said many of them are all right. The principles that you refer to are right but how this can harmonize with your pointed remarks to Dr. Waggoner, I cannot see. I think you are too sharp. And then when this is followed by a pamphlet published of your own views, be assured I cannot feel that you are just right at this point to do this unless you give the same liberty to Dr. Waggoner. Had you avoided the question, which you state has been done, it would have been more in accordance with the light God has seen fit to give to me. . . .

I tell you brethren I am troubled, when I see you take positions that you forbid others to take and that you would condemn in others. I do not think this is the right way to deal with one another. I want to see no pharisaism among us. The matter now has been brought so fully before the people by yourself as well as Dr. Waggoner, that it must be met fairly and squarely in open discussion. I see no other way and if this cannot be done without a spirit of pharisaism then let us stop publishing these matters and learn more fully lessons in the school of Christ. I believe now that nothing can be done but open discussion. You circulated your pamphlet, now it is only fair that Dr. Waggoner should have just as fair a chance as you have had. I think the whole thing is not in God's order. But brethren we must have no unfairness. We must work as Christians. If we have any point that is not fully, clearly defined and can bear the test of criticism don't be afraid or too proud to yield it.[37]

Mrs. White realized the matter could not be suppressed, so she called for a free and open forum. This discussion reached a confrontation at the historic Minneapolis conference in 1888.

37. White to Butler and Smith, 5 Apr. 1887, from Basel, Switzerland.

5

The Early Waggoner: 1887

E. J. Waggoner had not fully recovered the Protestant message of justification by faith by 1886. Much less had he recovered Paul's message of justification, which is eschatological as well as forensic. It may come as a shock to learn that although Waggoner believed in justification by faith alone, he taught that eternal life and salvation were based on successful lawkeeping—with God's help of course. If this primitive view of soteriology was light for Adventism, how great must have been the legal darkness! If God used Waggoner to bring light on the gospel to the church, then God was not shining the full blaze of even the imperfect Reformation light on the Adventist community.

Those who compare Waggoner's early gropings after the gospel with the clear doctrine of justification propounded by the best nineteenth-century Protestant scholars will be startled. They will be especially disturbed if they think this special "remnant" community had light on the gospel far in advance of "poor Babylonian Protestants."

In 1866 James Buchanan delivered a series of lectures on *The Doctrine of Justification: An Outline of Its History in the Church and of Its Exposition from Scripture*. Published in 1867, it remains one of the finest works on the subject written at any time or in any language. It makes Waggoner's presentation appear feebly immature. Charles Haddon Spurgeon, that prince of preachers, also knew how to divide law and gospel, justification and sanctification, grace and glory with masterful skill.

The little "remnant" had no great theologians or teachers like Buchanan, Spurgeon or Hodge. And until they could grow to mature New Testament faith, they would necessarily remain in comparative obscurity.

The idea that Waggoner had a message of righteousness by faith far in advance of the Reformers or Wesley would be amusing if it were not such a serious aberration. It betrays an Adventist triumphalism nourished on ignorance and isolationism. Unless we are willing to honestly look at our history and our actual gospel performance, we will live in a self-made "fool's paradise."

Until we know what grace is, we cannot endure to see ourselves as we actually are. Unless we believe in divine election, we cannot face the truth of our collective history. But honestly facing our miserable attempts to articulate the gospel should not cause us to lose faith in God's calling of the Advent movement. Election is not based on denominational goodness.

Waggoner was one of Adventism's greatest gospel preachers. But he did not compare with the great Protestant preachers of his time. When the early Adventists debated other religionists, they never engaged the great Westminster or Princeton scholars. They argued with Campbellites and those whose ideas on law and grace were so confused that Adventist teachers appeared bright by comparison. Seventh-day Adventism has

nerve a man to face anything (Rom. 8:30-39).

Although the Reformers recovered the judicial or forensic understanding of justification in Paul, they did not recover the glory of its eschatological meaning. In the Advent movement God restored the eschatological setting for the gospel (Rev. 14:6, 7). Here were a people who believed they faced the judgment—a judgment which demanded a righteousness of them which could stand before the face of God. The Adventist concepts of judgment, law and day of atonement provide a marvelous eschatological framework for preaching the gospel.

No one really understands the gospel until he can answer the question, On what basis is a man accepted in the final judgment? One who relegates justification merely to Christian initiation may talk of justification by Christ's imputed righteousness. But what has he gained if he then turns to an eschatological salvation by an indwelling righteousness. He has simply begun as a Protestant and ended as a Roman Catholic. And who could be sure he was ready for the judgment if the verdict of acquittal depended on the measure of his sanctification?

On February 10, 1887, Waggoner addressed the question of how a man is accepted in the judgment. He began by stating the certainty of the judgment. The law is the standard. It will demand nothing less than a righteousness commensurate with the righteousness of God. Said Waggoner:

> If we are ever at a loss to know how perfect the law requires us to be, we have only to consider the life and character of Jesus. He "did no sin, neither was guile found in his mouth." This was simply because the law was in his heart. Anyone who models his life in accordance with the law of God, will be just like Christ, and the law will be satisfied with nothing less.
>
> This righteousness cannot be attained by our own in-

> dividual effort. Of ourselves we can do nothing; but Christ, who knew no sin, was made to be sin for us, in order "that we might be made the righteousness of God *in him.*" And so the command to know that God will bring us into judgment for every secret thing, includes the command not only to know that the law of God is to be the standard of that judgment, but also that through Christ alone can we attain to that perfect righteousness which the law demands. If Christ dwells in our hearts by faith, then we can exhibit in our actions the righteousness of the law, for if we have Christ in the heart we must have the law there also. And having lived thus, when we are brought before the judgment-seat, and God fixes upon us his piercing gaze, he will see, not us, but the image of Christ, and because he lives we shall live also.[3]

This statement by Waggoner is disappointing. But let us not be too harsh on one who ranks among Adventism's most brilliant exponents of the gospel. His teaching on a believer's acceptance in the judgment was contrary to justification by faith. But the principles he was advocating on the law and the gospel would have eventually corrected that misunderstanding. The great Reformation historian, Philip Schaff, once said that Luther understood justification by faith in his heart long before he could clearly articulate it.[4] When the young Reformer was shaking Europe with the gospel, he believed in prayers for the dead, the mass, "good" indulgences and the authority of the pope, and could still enunciate only an Augustinian view of justification by

---

3. E. J. Waggoner, "Things We Should Know," no. 2, *Signs of the Times*, 10 Feb. 1887, p. 86.

4. "He [Luther] was gradually brought to the conviction that the sinner is justified by faith alone, without works of law. He experienced this truth in his heart long before he understood it in all its bearings" (Philip Schaff, *History of the Christian Church*, 7:122).

faith.[5] But the early Luther possessed the ingredients which were to explode his own errors and break the stranglehold of the papacy. Likewise, Waggoner's light on the law and the gospel contained the vital ingredients to explode his own errors and to lighten the earth with the glory of God.

---

5. In its essence Augustine's conception of salvation is the "renewal of man by grace which enables him to become righteous by doing good works in love, for man is justified by faith which works through love. The emphasis is on love, which is the actual content of justification" (Uuras Saarnivaara, *Luther Discovers the Gospel*, p. 17). For a detailed discussion of Augustine's conception of the sinner's salvation and its relation to Luther's mature teaching on justification, see pp. 3-18.

6

Waggoner's 1888 Message

Waggoner's name will always be associated with justification by faith and the Minneapolis conference of 1888. Mrs. White declared it was the beginning of the light which was to propel the little Advent body into the latter rain and loud cry. If accepted, the 1888 message would have brought the speedy finishing of God's work on earth. If Mrs. White is to be believed, the appallingly simple fact is that Minneapolis itself explains why Christ has not come. The issue of that conference has returned to the Seventh-day Adventist church with new urgency. The burning question is, What did Waggoner actually present in 1888? We have no record of Waggoner and Jones' actual presentations. Uriah Smith, however, briefly summarized the first three of Waggoner's eleven studies. Here is his report as it appeared in the *General Conference Daily Bulletin*:

Wednesday, October 17, 1888

At 2:30 p.m. Elder E. J. Waggoner discussed the question of the law of God and its relation to the Gospel of Christ. The discussion was based principally on the Epistle to the Romans.[1]

Thursday, October 18, 1888

At 9 a.m. Elder E. J. Waggoner gave another lesson on the law and gospel. In this lesson the first and second chapters of Galatians, in connection with Acts 15, were partially presented by him to show that the same harmony existed there as elsewhere; that the key to the book was "justification by faith in Christ," with the emphasis on the latter word; that liberty in Christ was always freedom from sin, and that separation from Christ to some other means of justification always brought bondage. He stated incidentally that "the law of Moses" and "the law of God" were not distinctive terms as applied to the ceremonial and moral laws, and cited Num. xv., 22-24, and Luke ii., 23-24, as proof. He closed at 10:15 by asking those present to compare Acts xv., 7-11, with Rom. ii., 20-25. Appeals were made by Brother Waggoner and Sister White to the brethren, old and young, to seek God, put away all spirit of prejudice and opposition, and strive to come into the unity of faith in the bonds of brotherly love.[2]

---

1. Uriah Smith, "First Day's Proceedings," *General Conference Daily Bulletin* 2, no. 1 (19 Oct. 1888): 2.

2. Uriah Smith, "Second Day's Proceedings," *General Conference Daily Bulletin* 2, no. 1 (19 Oct. 1888): 2.

Friday, October 19, 1888

At 9 a.m. Elder Waggoner continued his lessons on the law and gospel. The Scriptures considered were the fifteenth chapter of Acts and the second and third of Galatians, compared with Romans iv. and other passages in Romans. His purpose was to show that the real point of controversy was justification by faith in Christ, which faith is reckoned to us as to Abraham, for righteousness. The covenant and promises to Abraham are the covenant and promises to us.[3]

Waggoner's series continued until Thursday, October 25. Uriah Smith then wrote this summarizing comment:

A series of instructive lectures has been given on "Justification by faith" by Eld. E. J. Waggoner. The closing one was given this morning. With the foundation principles all are agreed, but there are some differences in regard to the interpretation of several passages. The lectures have tended to a more thorough investigation of the truth, and it is hoped that the unity of the faith will be reached on this important question.[4]

Of considerable interest is Waggoner's synopsis of both Jones' and his own lectures in the November 2, 1888, issue of the *Signs of the Times*.

The principal subjects of Bible study were the ten kingdoms into which, according to the prophecy, the Roman Empire was divided, the establishment of the Papacy, and of its counterpart, the proposed National Reform Government; and the law and the gospel in their

---

3. Uriah Smith, "Third Day's Proceedings," *General Conference Daily Bulletin* 2, no. 2 (21 Oct. 1888): 1.

4. Uriah Smith, "Eighth Day's Proceedings," *General Conference Daily Bulletin* 2, no. 7 (26 Oct. 1888): 3.

> various relations, coming under the general head of justification by faith. These subjects have aroused a deep interest in the minds of all present; and thus far during the Conference one hour a day has been devoted to a continuance of their study.[5]

However, the lack of a complete record of Waggoner's presentation has made it easy for some to read their own particular views on righteousness by faith into the 1888 conference.

Robert J. Wieland has a special affection for *The Glad Tidings*, Waggoner's commentary on Paul's Epistle to the Galatians. This was first published in the *Signs of the Times* in 1898-1899 as a series entitled "Studies in Galatians." It was repeated in the *Review* and finally published as a book in 1900. In 1972 it was reprinted by the Pacific Press Publishing Association after Wieland had editorially removed some pantheistic statements.

The myth that *The Glad Tidings* of 1900 represents the 1888 message has been promoted by the advertising on the back cover of the 1972 reprint. Here Waggoner's 1888 lectures on Galatians are virtually identified with his 1900 commentary revised by Wieland. This myth seems to suggest, "Do you want to know all about the 1888 message? Then read *The Glad Tidings*!"

Froom fostered a similar myth when he proposed that some of the works published after 1888 presented the light that began to break at the conference. Froom, of course, did not originate this myth. A. G. Daniells apparently felt that Waggoner's 1891 studies on Romans,[6] or even his pantheistic book, *The Everlasting Covenant*,

---

5. E. J. Waggoner, "Editorial Correspondence," *Signs of the Times*, 2 Nov. 1888, p. 662.

6. Arthur G. Daniells, in *General Conference Bulletin*, 1901, p. 272; cited in LeRoy E. Froom, *Movement of Destiny*, p. 263.

were the light of 1888.[7]

These myths are based on a common fallacy. They look to Waggoner's subsequent works for evidence of what he taught in 1888. Some clues can be found in these works. But Waggoner's writings prior to 1888, and especially his articles written on the verge of the conference, basically represent his presentations at that time.

Before 1888 Waggoner had been writing extensively on the law in Galatians and its connection with justification by faith. As mentioned earlier, a controversy on the law in Galatians had flared between him and George Butler. Butler had written a book to refute Waggoner.[8] And Waggoner had replied in a seventy-one page open letter dated February 10, 1887.[9] He released this for publication one month after the Minneapolis conference, presumably because Mrs. White had decided that the controversy over the law in Galatians should be settled by fair and open discussion.[10]

---

7. A. V. Olson, *Through Crisis to Victory: 1888-1901*, p. 231. *The Everlasting Covenant* was written by E. J. Waggoner and not by J. H. Waggoner as Olson suggests.

8. George I. Butler, *The Law in the Book of Galatians: Is It the Moral Law, or Does It Refer to that System of Laws Peculiarly Jewish?*

9. E. J. Waggoner, *The Gospel in the Book of Galatians: A Review.*

10. Writing to Butler and Smith, Mrs. White declared:

"I tell you brethren I am troubled, when I see you take positions that you forbid others to take and that you would condemn in others. I do not think this is the right way to deal with one another. I want to see no pharisaism among us. The matter now has been brought so fully before the people by yourself as well as Dr. Waggoner, that it must be met fairly and squarely in open discussion. I see no other way and if this cannot be done without a spirit of pharisaism then let us stop publishing these matters and learn more fully lessons in the school of Christ. I believe now that nothing can be done but open discussion. You circulated your pamphlet, now it is only fair that Dr. Waggoner should have just as fair a chance as you have had. I think the whole thing is not in God's order. But brethren we must have no unfairness. We must work as Christians. If we have any point that is not fully, clearly defined and can bear the test of criticism don't be afraid or too proud to yield it" (White to Butler and Smith, 5 Apr. 1887).

Uriah Smith's report on Waggoner's presentation at the conference confirms that his subject was the law in Galatians in connection with justification by faith.[11] This agrees with Mrs. White's recollection of Dr. Waggoner's studies.

> "The law was our schoolmaster to bring us unto Christ, that we might be justified by faith" (Gal. 3:24). In this scripture, the Holy Spirit through the apostle is speaking especially of the moral law. The law reveals sin to us, and causes us to feel our need of Christ and to flee unto Him for pardon and peace by exercising repentance toward God and faith toward our Lord Jesus Christ.
>
> An unwillingness to yield up preconceived opinions, and to accept this truth, lay at the foundation of a large share of the opposition manifested at Minneapolis against the Lord's message through Brethren [E. J.] Waggoner and [A. T.] Jones.[12]
>
> I see the beauty of truth in the presentation of the righteousness of Christ in relation to the law as the doctor has placed it before us. You say, many of you, it is light and truth. Yet you have not presented it in this light heretofore. Is it not possible that through earnest, prayerful searching of the Scriptures he has seen still greater light on some points? That which has been presented harmonizes perfectly with the light which God has been pleased to give me during all the years of my experience. If our ministering brethren would accept the doctrine which has been presented so clearly—the righteousness of Christ in connection with the law—and I know they need to accept this, their prejudices would not have a controlling power, and the people would be fed with their portion of meat in due season.[13]

---

11. See notes 1-4.

12. Ellen G. White, *Selected Messages*, 1:234.

13. Ellen G. White, Manuscript 15, 1888; cited in Olson, *Crisis to Victory*, p. 295.

It is obvious that what had preoccupied a man up to the time of the conference and what he himself had published one month after the conference would provide the clue to what he presented at the conference.

Just before the conference of 1888 Waggoner clearly taught a purely forensic justification. In the year of that conference he wrote two articles in the *Signs* which demonstrate his reliance on Luther and show that he was moving toward the recovery of the Reformation doctrine of justification by faith. These two articles, we believe, hold the key to the light of 1888.

Two Kinds of Righteousness

On February 24, 1888, Waggoner published an article entitled "Different Kinds of Righteousness."[14] He obviously received his inspiration for this article from Luther. In fact, he quoted rather extensively from Luther's *Commentary on Galatians*.

Waggoner's basic thesis was that there are two kinds of righteousness—Christ's righteousness, also called the righteousness of faith, and our righteousness, which is the righteousness of the law. The connection between this theme and Luther will be obvious to those acquainted with the birth of the Protestant Reformation.

According to Luther's own testimony, it was in 1519 that he came to a Reformational understanding of "the

14. E. J. Waggoner, "Different Kinds of Righteousness," *Signs of the Times*, 24 Feb. 1888, p. 119.

righteousness of God" and justification by faith.[15] Early in that year Luther wrote his pathfinding sermon on *Two Kinds of Righteousness*.[16] One righteousness was the infinite righteousness of Christ, His suffering and dying for us. The other righteousness was the godly life of the believer. Luther was not yet able to articulate his doctrine of righteousness by faith in terms of imputed or forensic righteousness. And not everything in his sermon represents the clear Protestant doctrine. But as John Dillenberger's selections from Martin Luther's writings demonstrate, this sermon on *Two Kinds of Righteousness* was the basic structure on which Luther built his Reformation theology.[17] Luther's great *Commentary on Galatians* shows that he built everything around this basic distinction between gospel righteous-

---

15. Martin Luther, *Luther's Works*, 34:334-37. A confederacy of liberal, ecumenical and Roman Catholic Luther scholars have tried to prove that Luther came to the Reformation understanding much earlier. Recently, however, the best Luther scholarship has vindicated Luther's own testimony on the dating of his breakthrough into the Reformation light. See esp. Lowell C. Green, "Faith, Righteousness and Justification: New Light on Their Development under Luther and Melanchthon," *Sixteenth Century Journal* 4, no. 1 (Apr. 1973): 65-86. Also of value is Green's article, "Luther Research in English-Speaking Countries Since 1971," *Lutherjahrbuch* 44 (1977), esp. pp. 110-12. See also William C. Robinson, *The Reformation: A Rediscovery of Grace*, pp. 89-90.

16. John Dillenberger, ed., *Martin Luther: Selections from His Writings*, pp. 86-96.

17. Ibid., pp. xvii-xix.

ness and law righteousness.[18]

In his Galatians commentary Luther called the first righteousness "passive righteousness," "gospel righteousness," "the righteousness of faith," "imputed righteousness." The second he called "active righteousness," "good works" and "the righteousness of the law." The first righteousness is not a quality in the heart, for the heart possesses it only in faith. But the second is a quality, for it consists in love and good works by the power of the Holy Spirit.

This clear distinction—but not separation—between gospel and law, justification and sanctification, was the Magna Charta of the Reformation. As Dr. Lowell C. Green demonstrates, this was the great hermeneutic principle of the Reformation.[19] Luther declared that whoever blurs or destroys that distinction blurs or destroys the light of the Reformation.

Waggoner had been moving toward the recovery of Reformation theology since 1884. But his article on "Different Kinds of Righteousness" shows he had not fully penetrated the Reformation position. Waggoner apparently thought the righteousness of the law refers only to

---

18. Martin Luther, *A Commentary on St. Paul's Epistle to the Galatians*. First published in 1535, these lectures perhaps show Luther at his best. One of the works of Luther to be translated into English during the sixteenth century, it appeared in 1575 and again in 1578. This translation has been reissued in about thirty various editions. The most recent and perhaps the most satisfying was prepared by Philip Watson in 1953. See also Luther, *Luther's Works*, 26-27. In his *Grace Abounding to the Chief of Sinners*, John Bunyan (1628-1688), who was languishing in jail, told how a long time before this "the God in whose hands are all our days and ways, did cast into my hand, one day, a book of Martin Luther's. It was his comment on the Galatians . . . [the] which, when I had but a little way perused, I found my condition in his experience, so largely and profoundly handled as if his book had been written out of my heart. . . . I do prefer this book of Martin Luther's upon the Galatians (excepting the Holy Bible) before all the books that ever I have seen, as most fit for a wounded conscience."

19. Green, "Faith, Righteousness and Justification."

efforts to keep the law by unaided human effort. He failed to see that "the righteousness of the law" (Rom. 8:4) also refers to genuine sanctification, which the Bible does call "our righteousness" (Deut. 6:25), "his [the believer's] righteousness" (Ezek. 3:20), "your good works" (Matt. 5:16), "mine own righteousness" (Phil. 3:9) and "your work of faith" and "labour of love" (1 Thess. 1:3).[20] In other words, what Luther called "active righteousness" refers to the sanctified living of the believer. This must not be confused with passive righteousness—the righteousness of faith.

Although Waggoner distinguished "our righteousness" "of the law" from the righteousness of faith, his distinction did not go far enough. He failed to see that works done after grace as well as before grace must be excluded from the article of the saving righteousness of faith. Otherwise sanctification can be included in the righteousness of faith. Salvation is then based partly on what Christ has done and partly on what the believer does.[21]

---

20. Speaking of the righteousness of the law, the Lutheran Reformer, Martin Chemnitz, wrote:

"For the righteousness of the Law is that a man does the things that are written in the Law; but the righteousness of faith is by believing to appropriate to oneself what Christ has done for us. Therefore the works by which the regenerate do those things which are written in the Law, either before or after their renewal, belong to the righteousness of the Law, though some in one way, others in another. . . .

"The obedience of Christ is imputed to us for righteousness. That glory cannot be taken away from Christ and transferred to either our renewal or our obedience without blasphemy" (Martin Chemnitz, *Examination of the Council of Trent*, Part 1, pp. 490-91).

21. Just by saying that Christ does the lawkeeping in the believer is not a magic wand to relieve the problem, because the believer does have a part in living the Christian life. In fact, saying that Christ does the obeying in the believer compounds the error because it blurs the distinction between the Creator and the creature in sanctification. This is really, as we will demonstrate later, a pantheistic principle.

Waggoner's February 24 article on "Different Kinds of Righteousness," however, gave conclusive evidence that he was struggling to grasp the light which broke mightily on the world in the sixteenth century.[22] This, of course, belies the claim that Waggoner was far in advance of the Reformation.

In July, 1888, three months before the Minneapolis conference, Waggoner gave further evidence that he was struggling to recover the light given to Luther. He wrote a significant article, entitled "Lawful Use of the Law," in which he quoted extensively from Luther.[23] This article provides greater insight into Waggoner's contribution to the doctrine of justification by faith than anything else he wrote.

In order to understand the significance of Waggoner's use of Luther, we need to reflect on the law in Reformation history. Melanchthon was the first Reformation theologian to define what became known as the three uses of the law:

1. In the social use the knowledge of the law acts as a restraint on sin and for the promotion of right doing in society.

2. In the pedagogic use the law brings man under the conviction of sin, makes him conscious of his inability to meet the demands of the law, works wrath and acts as a tutor to bring him to Christ.

3. In the didactic or normative use, also called the *tertius usus legis* or third use of the law, the law becomes a

---

22. As did his letter to Butler, February 10, 1887, published as *The Gospel in the Book of Galatians: A Review*, probably in December, 1888.

23. E. J. Waggoner, "Lawful Use of the Law," *Signs of the Times*, 13 July 1888, p. 422.

rule of life for the believer after he is justified. It reminds him of his duty and leads him in the way of life and salvation.

In teaching the gospel and justification unto life eternal, the law is used as the "schoolmaster" (Gal. 3:24) to drive us to Christ that we might be justified by faith. But it is the third use of the law that teaches the true way of sanctification.

The church before the Reformation was much like the Adventist community before 1888. All the emphasis was placed on the third use of the law. Men tried to obtain life by keeping the law—with God's help of course! They thought they could finally stand in the judgment if they kept the law well enough or if Christ kept it in them—really the same in principle. But no one could be sure of salvation or acceptance in the final judgment, for no one could be sure he was keeping the law to the full satisfaction of divine justice.

Luther's great emphasis was the second use of the law, especially in his *Commentary on Galatians*.[24] With powerful assaults on the legalism of the church, Luther showed it was vain to expect life from the law "before grace or after grace." The law works wrath (Rom. 4:15). Its office for fallen man is not to give life but to terrify, to kill and to hammer all human righteousness into powder. Luther's emphasis on this use of the law was so great that his lectures on Galatians seem to have a negative attitude to the law. In the same way, the careless reader might also think Paul speaks against the law in passages like Romans 7 and Galatians 3.

In Adventism nearly all the emphasis was placed on

---

24. Luther often referred to St. Paul's Epistle to the Galatians as "my Katie von Bora," for he treasured this book of the Bible with special affection.

the third use of the law. This is not surprising since the Adventist mission was to urge obedience to all the Ten Commandments. Many apparently took considerable satisfaction in the thought that they alone were God's favored "remnant" because they kept all God's commandments. Even men like Smith, Butler and, yes, Waggoner, rested in the hope that successful lawkeeping would enable men to finally stand in judgment and win the verdict of eternal life. Even what Mrs. White had said before 1888 was insufficient to expose this vain Laodicean hope.[25]

Waggoner came to this law-loving, law-boasting community like a Martin Luther. He unveiled the fierce face of the law in its terrible greatness, its wrath against imperfection and its righteousness that can only condemn and never justify the sinner. Adventists had evaded the force of Galatians 3 by saying Paul was only discussing the ritual law. They could not bear the fierce face of the moral law, which tore their Laodicean righteousness to shreds. To Smith and Butler it seemed that Waggoner's position on the law in Galatians would pull down the pillars of the Advent faith and weaken its stand on the Ten Commandments. Before leaving for Minneapolis Waggoner fired Martin Luther's words on the use of the law at his would-be opposition.[26]

Again, this resort to Luther explodes the myth that Waggoner was far in advance of the sixteenth-century Reformation. The facts of history reveal that the little

---

25. The inspiration that God gives to a charismatic leader must be viewed as progressive. God accommodates this gift to the situation of His people. Ellen G. White shows evidence that she progressed into an ever clearer grasp of the gospel. Her earlier statements on justification by faith are not nearly as clear as her post-1888 articles.

26. He was obviously carrying on his argument with Butler and Smith in the columns of the *Signs of the Times*.

Adventist community were reliving the controversy of the sixteenth century. They had the opportunity to rediscover what the Reformers had said long before them. When Luther began preaching justification by faith, his Roman Catholic opponents argued that Paul's disparaging remarks on the law as a method of salvation referred to the ceremonial law rather than the moral law. The Adventist understanding of the law before 1888 was like the church's view of the law before the Reformation.

Waggoner's discovery that the moral law was the particular issue in Romans and Galatians 3 was part of the heritage of the Protestant Reformation. There is no evidence, however, that he ever fully recovered that heritage. What might have been the blessing if his brethren had heartily joined him in a corporate recovery of the gospel—a recovery far exceeding the light of the Reformation! But this was not to be. Waggoner was part of his community. He could not transcend its limitations. Did he try to press on alone, only to stumble and fall?

We have shown why we believe that Waggoner's pre-1888 material best represents his mind at the conference. All the available evidence confirms this. The great issue at the conference was the law in Galatians. It involved Waggoner's recovery of the Reformation heritage on the second use of the law. The light was unwelcome.

Wieland's suggestion that the central issue at Minneapolis was justification by faith and that the argument on the law in Galatians was only a distraction is another myth.[27] Just as Luther's use of law was an integral part of his message on justification, so the use of the law was an essential part of Waggoner's message on

27. See A. L. Hudson, ed., *A Warning and Its Reception*, p. 71.

justification. Luther's message was law and gospel. And from 1884 to 1888 law and gospel was Waggoner's constant theme.

Ellen G. White understood that Waggoner's light at Minneapolis was light on the relation of the law to the gospel. She commented that this light was to lighten the earth with the glory of God (Rev. 18:1).[28] Mrs. White was impressed with Waggoner's message on the law and the gospel when she first heard him at Minneapolis. She

---

28. Let the reader consider carefully the evidence of the following remarks of Ellen G. White:

"The law was our schoolmaster to bring us unto Christ, that we might be justified by faith" (Gal. 3:24). In this scripture, the Holy Spirit through the apostle is speaking especially of the moral law. The law reveals sin to us, and causes us to feel our need of Christ and to flee unto Him for pardon and peace by exercising repentance toward God and faith toward our Lord Jesus Christ.

"An unwillingness to yield up preconceived opinions, and to accept this truth, lay at the foundation of a large share of the opposition manifested at Minneapolis against the Lord's message through Brethren [E. J.] Waggoner and [A. T.] Jones. By exciting that opposition Satan succeeded in shutting away from our people, in a great measure, the special power of the Holy Spirit that God longed to impart to them. The enemy prevented them from obtaining that efficiency which might have been theirs in carrying the truth to the world, as the apostles proclaimed it after the day of Pentecost. The light that is to lighten the whole earth with its glory was resisted, and by the action of our own brethren has been in a great degree kept away from the world" (White, *Selected Messages*, 1:234-35).

responded with her whole being[29]—even though there were some points on which she thought Waggoner may have been wrong.[30] Significantly, after 1888 she made the second use of the law more prominent.[31]

The Uriah Smith–Ellen G. White Misunderstanding

Uriah Smith was distressed when this "mother in Israel" took E. J. Waggoner's position on the law in Galatians. He had expected her to take the same position she did in the similar controversy with Waggoner's

---

29. "Dr. Waggoner . . . has presented his views in a plain, straightforward manner, as a Christian should. . . .

"I have no reason to think that he is not as much esteemed of God as are any of my brethren. . . .

"I know it would be dangerous to denounce Dr. Waggoner's position as wholly erroneous. . . . I see the beauty of truth in the presentation of the righteousness of Christ in relation to the law as the doctor has placed it before us. . . . That which has been presented harmonizes perfectly with the light which God has been pleased to give me during all the years of my experience. If our ministering brethren would accept the doctrine which has been presented so clearly—the righteousness of Christ in connection with the law—and I know they need to accept this . . . " (White, Manuscript 15, 1888; cited in Olson, *Crisis to Victory*, pp. 294-95).

"When I stated before my brethren that I had heard for the first time the views of Elder E. J. Waggoner, some did not believe me. I stated that I had heard precious truths uttered that I could respond to with all my heart, for had not these great and glorious truths, the righteousness of Christ and the entire sacrifice made in behalf of man, been imprinted indelibly upon my mind by the Spirit of God? . . . When the Lord had given to my brethren [Waggoner and Jones] the burden to proclaim this message I felt inexpressibly grateful to God, for I knew it was a message for this time" (Ellen G. White, Manuscript 24, 1888).

30. In her closing address at Minneapolis, Ellen G. White stated: "Some interpretations of Scripture given by Dr. Waggoner I do not regard as correct" (White, Manuscript 15, 1888; cited in Olson, *Crisis to Victory*, p. 294). One example that she probably had in mind was Waggoner's interpretation of the phrase in Galatians 3:19, "till the Seed should come to whom the promise was made." Waggoner believed that this referred to the second advent of Christ.

31. White, *Selected Messages*, 1:233-41, 341, 367.

father in 1856. Her apparent about-face astonished him. What is more, Mrs. White had sent a testimony telling J. H. Waggoner he was wrong.

There is another interesting aspect to this matter. In her February 18, 1887, letter to Waggoner and Jones, written from Basel, Switzerland, Mrs. White said the dispute over the law in Galatians was an unimportant side issue which should not disturb the unity of the church. But when she actually heard Waggoner on this disputed matter in 1888, she thought it was worth risking a denominational revolution.

A little over a year after Minneapolis, Uriah Smith wrote a letter to Mrs. White on the issue of the law in Galatians. He expressed considerable surprise at the change in her position. He reminded her of the 1856 debate over J. H. Waggoner's position, of her part in silencing him and of her testimony to J. H. Waggoner stating he was wrong. Smith stated that E. J. Waggoner's articles in the *Signs* of 1886 had seemed to him then, as well as at the time of writing in February, 1890, to directly contradict Mrs. White's counsel to J. H. Waggoner.

According to Smith some had tried to make it appear that Mrs. White did not have J. H. Waggoner's stand on the law in Galatians in mind when she said his position was wrong. Smith was adamant, however, that the only issue involved in 1856 was whether the law which Paul said was "added" was the moral law.[32]

Mrs. White, however, was not as clear on the subject as Smith appeared to be. In her February, 1887, letter to Waggoner and Jones, she said:

> I have been looking in vain as yet for an article that was

---

32. Smith to White, 17 Feb. 1890; Smith to W. A. McCutchen, 8 Aug. 1901.

> written nearly twenty years ago [1867] in reference to the "added law." I read this to Elder [J. H.] Waggoner. I stated then to him that I had been shown that his position in regard to the law was incorrect, and from the statement I made to him he has been silent upon the subject for many years. . . .
>
> I have sent repeatedly for my writings on the law, but that special article has not yet appeared. There is such an article in Healdsburg, I am well aware, but it has not come as yet. I have much writing many years old on the law, but the special article I read to Elder Waggoner has not come to me. . . .
>
> I have wanted to get out articles in regard to the law, but I have been moving about so much, my writings are where I can not have advantage of them. . . . But I did see years ago that Elder Waggoner's views were not correct, and read to him matter which I had written.[33]

About seven weeks later Mrs. White wrote Butler and Smith, reiterating her deep concern over the loss of the article she had read to J. H. Waggoner. She said:

> I am troubled; for the life of me, I cannot remember that which I have been shown in reference to the two laws. I cannot remember what the caution and warning referred to were, that were given to Elder Waggoner. It may be it was a caution not to make his ideas prominent at that time, for there was great danger of disunion.[34]

Mrs. White's ambivalent recollections on this matter make us wonder whether she told J. H. Waggoner that his views were wrong or whether she was only trying to caution him against agitating differences among the brethren. Smith, however, wrote to Mrs. White, saying:

> My recollection on that is quite distinct, and if I was on

---

33. Ellen G. White, Letter 37, 1887.
34. White to Butler and Smith, 5 Apr. 1887.

> oath at a court of justice, I should be obliged to testify that to the best of my knowledge and belief, that was the only point then at issue [whether the law in Galatians 3 was the Ten Commandments or the Mosaic law system]; and on that you [Ellen G. White] said that Brother Waggoner was wrong.[35]

In a letter written in response to Mrs. White's rebuke for his *Signs* articles of 1886, E. J. Waggoner added to the apparent confusion when he said:

> I will say also that I had never heard of your having read a testimony to my father in regard to the law. I did not know that you had ever spoken on the subject. If I had known that, the case would have been different.

He then added: "I may state, however, that the view which I have taught is quite materially different from that which father held. I do not know whether or not he now holds the same view."[36] However, an examination of J. H. Waggoner's book, *The Law of God: An Examination of the Testimony of Both Testaments*, shows that he and his son took substantially the same position on the

---

35. Smith to White, 17 Feb. 1890.

36. Our attempts to locate the original of this letter have failed. The only remaining evidence for its existence is found in a letter from Dores E. Robinson to W. H. Branson, dated May 8, 1935. On pages 3 and 4 of this letter Robinson quotes from E. J. Waggoner's letter, adding the following comment: "I have copied this from the original which we have on our correspondence file at the office." At the time of writing the letter, Robinson was on the staff of the Ellen G. White Estate in Washington, D.C.

law in Galatians 3.[37] Why then did E. J. Waggoner plead that his position differed from his father's? Was it to protect himself from the charge of guilt by association? Or was it a wish to be judged on his own merits? Furthermore, what happened to the testimony Mrs. White wrote to father J. H. Waggoner, saying he was wrong? No one seems to know.

Some conservatives will think it irreverent to raise these problems. But with their rigid view of "spiritual gifts," some have virtually dehumanized Mrs. White. Is

---

37. Some representative statements from J. H. Waggoner's book, *The Law of God: An Examination of the Testimony of Both Testaments* (1854), are as follows.

Regarding the circumstances under which the Apostle Paul wrote the Epistle to the Galatians, J. H. Waggoner stated:

"His declaration of what he said to Peter at Antioch, some six years before, shows that they had been troubled with judaizing teachers, who did not understand that justification was obtained wholly through Christ 'without the law.' Rom. iii, 19-23. This is also shown in Gal. iv, 21; v, 1-4, but this does not prove that they were Jews to whom he wrote, or that judaism was the only error with which they were in danger of being affected" (p. 74).

On Galatians 3:2-5:

"It might be inferred from Gal. iii, 2-5, that he is no longer speaking of the moral law; but we must remember that justification cannot be obtained by a law, however holy and just it may be, after it is transgressed; and those who receive the Spirit, or work miracles, must necessarily do so by faith, and not by the works of the law" (p. 76).

On Galatians 3:24:

"When we inquire into the nature and office of the law that was added, there will be no difficulty in viewing it as the same that was transgressed. The law was added to serve as a school-master to bring us unto Christ, that we might be justified through faith: justification by the law being impossible by reason of transgression. Here it is evident that he refers to the moral law; for none but a moral law could bring us to Christ. He is the only Saviour from sin; and as the sick need a physician, so the sinful need a Saviour. But in order that the sinner come to Christ, he must be made sensible of his sinful condition; this can be done only by the law; for 'by the law is the knowledge of sin.' So 'the law of the Lord is perfect, converting the soul;' perfect as a standard of right, convincing of sin, and thus bringing us to Christ, the way of salvation. Such conversion is genuine and complete. Thus it is evident that the law spoken of in Gal. iii, 19, 24, is a moral law, one that will detect and convince of sin" (p. 81).

there not a danger in assuming personal infallibility in all she did? Regardless of the answers to these questions, Mrs. White emerges in our research as more human and more resourceful than many have thought. She was one of the few who enlarged their theological boundaries after the age of sixty.

As for Waggoner, he had already done the work for which he was born. We will see that his star never rose any higher.

On the phrase, "under the law":

"All will admit that the Galatians had been affected with Judaizing notions of self-righteousness; yet we trust it has been made plain that other errors were obtaining among them, having no reference to the customs of the Jews. If they 'turned back' to their former practices they would again become heathen idolaters; but if under the influence of other teachers they resorted to circumcision, and looked to the law for justification, they were also under condemnation, being proved sinners by their own rule of justification, and this is the signification of the phrase, 'under the law,' as used in the letters to the Romans and Galatians.... This, we think, plainly shows that the Apostle was convincing them of sin by the moral law" (p. 86).

Only the moral law is a rule of justification:

"Was any one, under any circumstances, justified by the law of Moses, or was justification ever coupled with that law? We think not. Nothing but a moral law can be a rule of justification; and the law of Moses consisted only in shadows, which were remembrancers of sin, but could never take away sin. They were not instituted as a means of acceptance with God, [see Ps. xl, 6-8; l, 8-12; Isa. ii, 10-20; Jer. vi, 20; Amos v, 21-24; 1 Sam. xv, 21, 22; Heb. viii, 5; ix, 9; x, 1-4,] and were not included in man's *whole duty* to him; [Jer. vii, 22, 23; Eccl. xii, 13;]" (p. 111).

7

Waggoner in Transition: 1889-1891

The years between the Minneapolis conference and Waggoner's departure for England in 1892 are fascinating years in his theological development. They furnish the clearest evidence of a theology in transition. In this period Waggoner did not express the pantheistic sentiments which appeared soon after his arrival in England. But in 1889-1891 he advanced theological positions which effectively laid the basis for his later pantheism. If we can give any credence to Waggoner's own *Confession*, written shortly before his death in 1916, he had privately abandoned faith in the Adventist doctrine of the cleansing of a heavenly sanctuary as early as 1891.[1]

Waggoner's writings between 1889 and 1891 are not difficult to analyze. He concentrated on justification by faith, the divinity and humanity of Christ, the meaning of the blood of Christ, living by faith and the righteous-

1. E. J. Waggoner, *A "Confession of Faith,"* pp. 14-15.

ness of God. In our analysis of Waggoner in transition, we will begin with the development of his new position on justification. This was central. We will then show how the other concepts were more or less supportive.

Justification by Faith

Before the 1888 conference Waggoner held a Protestant meaning of justification. He believed that justification was a forensic act in which God pronounces the believer righteous on the ground of the imputed righteousness of Christ. Furthermore, the Waggoner of 1888 distinguished between justification as a forensic act for the believer and sanctification as an effective act within the believer.

In 1889 and 1890 Waggoner wrote a series of articles in the *Signs*. Most of them were based on the book of Romans. Some of these articles were later incorporated into his best-known book, *Christ and His Righteousness.*

In these articles Waggoner began to adopt an "effective" justification.[2] At first he did not abandon forensic justification, a justification by imputed righteousness. But he took the position that justification is both a

2. In the history of theology, "forensic" and "effective" justification are terms which go back to the great battle over justification in the sixteenth century. Against the Reformers, who taught that the sinner is justified solely by the imputed righteousness of Christ (passive righteousness), the Romanists contended for that justification which is *justum efficere*. This expression may be translated as "make righteous." By insisting on this definition of justification, Rome confounded justification with sanctification, the forgiveness of the guilt of sins with the healing of the disease of sin, divine acceptance with spiritual attainment. In short, forensic justification means "to declare righteous," while effective justification means "to make righteous" by an internal renovation of character.

declaring just and a making just. This Roman principle quickly displaces the Protestant element. Thus, by 1891 Waggoner had replaced the Protestant doctrine of imputed righteousness with an internal work of grace. For him justification had become sanctification. Let us now trace this change in emphasis.

On February 4, 1889, Waggoner wrote an article entitled "The Obedience of Faith." Like Luther, he called imputed righteousness "passive righteousness" and the believer's new life of obedience "active righteousness." But after stating that "active righteousness is just as much the work of faith as is the other," he misused Philippians 3:9 and also called "active righteousness" righteousness by faith.[3] This was a fatal mistake.

Luther deliberately called one righteousness passive and the other active. Passive righteousness is what Christ did for us by His holy obedience two thousand years ago. It is counted as ours in the merciful reckoning of God. It is ours by faith alone. We had absolutely no part in working it out. This cannot be said of sanctification. Although God's Spirit works it in the believer, He does not obey for the believer. As a responsible person, the believer is called to meaningful human activity as he cooperates with God in the great work of overcoming. This righteousness is not passive but active. It involves what the believer himself does under the impulse of divine grace. This active righteousness is not called the righteousness of faith either in Paul or in Luther. Because Waggoner blurred their distinction and called them both righteousness by faith, he was logically forced to propose that the believer's new obedience of

---

3. E. J. Waggoner, "The Obedience of Faith," *Signs of the Times*, 4 Feb. 1889, p. 71.

faith "is not his personal action." Not long after this, Waggoner began saying it is God who does the believing and obeying in the believer. Blurring the distinction between the passive righteousness of faith and sanctification logically leads to blurring the distinction between God and the believer. And this is the essential premise of pantheism.

Waggoner had not yet developed his pantheism by February, 1889. But he possessed a logical mind that followed his premises through to their final end. When sanctification is confused with the righteousness of faith, one must logically contend that the righteous acts in the believer's life are the work of the Creator alone.

In April Waggoner confused the righteousness of faith (Phil. 3:9) with sanctification.[4] He even confused "the righteousness of God" (Rom. 1:17) with sanctification. In June, 1890, Waggoner correctly showed that eternal life is the reward of righteousness. But instead of showing that the substitutionary righteousness of Christ entitles the believer to eternal life, Waggoner argued that eternal life is the reward of an indwelling righteousness.[5]

In the same issue Waggoner presented direct evidence for his change to the Roman Catholic concept of "effective" justification.[6] He defined "to justify" as "to make righteous, or to show that one is already righteous." Waggoner correctly argued that the law can only justify a righteous man. But then he reasoned incorrectly that the sinner obtains the righteousness needed for his justi-

---

4. E. J. Waggoner, "'From Faith to Faith,'" *Signs of the Times*, 1 Apr. 1889, p. 199.

5. E. J. Waggoner, "According to His Deeds," *Signs of the Times*, 30 June 1890, p. 390.

6. E. J. Waggoner, "The Righteousness Which Is in the Law," *Signs of the Times*, 30 June 1890, p. 391.

fication when Christ imparts or creates this righteousness in him.

On September 8, 1890, Waggoner quoted Professor James R. Boise to support his interpretation that the Pauline doctrine of justification by imputed righteousness means justification by an infused righteousness. In Romans 3:22 the apostle declares that the righteousness by faith of Jesus Christ is unto all and upon all them that believe. Waggoner said:

> On the word rendered "unto," Prof. James R. Boise has this excellent note: "Not simply *unto*, in the sense of to, towards, up to, as the word is commonly understood; but *into* (in the strict and usual sense of *eis*), entering into the heart, into the inner being of *all those who have faith.*" This is exactly in accordance with God's promise in the covenant: "I will put My law in their inward parts, and write it in their hearts." Jer. 31:33. The righteousness that comes by faith is not superficial; it is actual; it is made a part of the individual.[7]

In his article, "The Blessing of Abraham," Waggoner pursued his false premise and confused the forgiveness of sins with the actual infusion of righteousness into the heart. He still used the term "imputed righteousness" but said that "it is righteousness put *into* and *upon* the sinner. That is, he is made righteous both inside and outside."[8] This is the old Roman Catholic error of utterly confounding justification and sanctification, forgiveness of sins and healing from sin.

If Waggoner only taught that forgiveness has sancti-

---

7. E. J. Waggoner, "How Righteousness Is Obtained," *Signs of the Times*, 8 Sept. 1890, p. 474.

8. E. J. Waggoner, "The Blessing of Abraham," *Signs of the Times*, 29 Sept. 1890, p. 497.

fying effects, there could be no valid objection. All great Protestant scholars consent to this. But careful reading of his material shows Waggoner had moved to an "effective" justification. He had made any distinction between justification and sanctification virtually meaningless.

At the end of 1890, in his pamphlet, *The Power of Forgiveness*, Waggoner introduced the mystical theory of atonement then becoming popular in some Protestant circles. Like John Henry Newman of Oxford Movement fame, Waggoner used this theory to support a justification which combines declaring righteous and making righteous. Equating blood with life, as in the mystical atonement, he reasoned that to be justified by Christ's blood means being justified by a mystical partaking of His life.[9] To be justified, therefore, means to be "made righteous, or doers of the law." When God declares a person righteous, He speaks Christ's righteousness or life "into and upon" him.

Waggoner occasionally used expressions like "impute," "reckon" and "accounted righteous." But the context provides no evidence that he meant that the righteousness of Jesus of Nazareth is accounted to us in God's merciful reckoning. Rather, he meant that the righteousness God puts into us and works in our hearts is counted as ours.

In the book, *Christ and His Righteousness*, adapted from his 1889-1890 *Signs* articles, Waggoner said justification means "to make righteous."[10] He also tended to confound forgiveness of sin with regeneration and healing from sin. This book, however, does not contain the more blatant Romanism of 1891. Waggoner still re-

---

9. E. J. Waggoner, *The Power of Forgiveness*, pp. 5-6.

10. E. J. Waggoner, *Christ and His Righteousness*, p. 51.

tained the concept of being justified and counted as though one had never sinned simply because Christ had borne the penalty of sin on the cross. Waggoner had not yet abandoned the truth of imputed righteousness, nor had he developed the mystical theory of atonement.

For Waggoner, however, it seemed that a little leaven of Roman Catholic justification soon leavened the whole lump. If his articles on justification in 1890 were disappointing, his lectures on Romans at the General Conference of 1891 were terrible.[11] Nothing of the Pauline and Reformation concept of justification remained. Waggoner's concept of justification in these lectures was wholly Roman Catholic. Justification was understood as an inward work of sanctifying the believer. Great Pauline texts referring to the vicarious righteousness of Christ were construed to mean an infused righteousness which makes the believer conformable to the law of God. Here is a sample of Waggoner's 1891 lectures.

> The prophet rejoiced in the Lord, because God had clothed him with the garments of salvation, and covered him with the robe of righteousness. We are not to put on the robe ourselves. Let us trust God to do that. When the Lord puts it on, it is not as an outward garment merely; but he puts it right through a man, so that he is all righteousness.[12]

> Justification is the law incarnate in Christ, put into the man, so it is incarnate in the man.[13]

> The forgiveness of sins is not simply a book transaction a wiping out of past accounts. It has a vital relation to the man himself. It is not a temporary work. Christ gives his

11. E. J. Waggoner, *Bible Studies on the Book of Romans.*
12. Ibid., p. 4.
13. Ibid., p. 5.

> righteousness, takes away the sin, and leaves his righteousness there, and that makes a radical change in the man.[14]
>
> ". . . being justified by faith," that is, being made conformable to the law by faith, "we have peace with God through our Lord Jesus Christ." The only way that man can be made conformable to the law, and live free from condemnation is by having faith in the promises of God. In Christ there is no unrighteousness, therefore there is nothing but righteousness. By believing on Christ, the Christian has the righteousness of Christ.[15]

Waggoner's studies on Romans thus reveal a marked departure from the Pauline and Reformation emphasis on forensic justification. Justification was interpreted as "to make righteous"—God's act of putting righteousness into a man's heart. The mighty gospel teaching that God counts the believer as if he were righteous because he looks to his Substitute was strangely absent from Waggoner's thinking. Commenting on Romans 5:19, he said: "If we have his [Christ's] life, we have a righteous life; his obedience works in us, and that makes us righteous. . . . It is not our obedience, but the obedience of Christ working in us."[16] These comments would be less objectionable if the subject matter were sanctification. But Romans 5:19 refers to the personal obedience of Christ on behalf of the human race.

In 1891 Waggoner apparently had no concept of the mediation of an "outside" righteousness. He was only concerned for an inward righteousness. This observation corresponds to his own *Confession* of 1916.

---

14. Ibid.
15. Ibid., p. 7.
16. Ibid., p. 15.

> Also, twenty-five years ago, . . . the self-evident truth that sin is not an entity but a condition that can exist only in a person, made it clear to me that it is impossible that there could be any such thing as the transferring of sins to the sanctuary in heaven, thus defiling that place; and that there could, consequently, be no such thing, either in 1844, A.D., or at any other time, as the "cleansing of the heavenly sanctuary."[17]

Waggoner failed to distinguish between guilt and uncleanness (if we may use sanctuary terminology). Being a legal debt, guilt is transferable. But the disease—sinful corruption—can only be healed. The Waggoner of 1891 had departed from the Protestant faith. By his own confession he was no longer an orthodox Adventist at heart. But the clearest evidence for his position is found in his lectures on Romans given to the General Conference of 1891.

It is even more disturbing that L. E. Froom could laud Waggoner's 1891 lectures and present them as evidence that righteousness by faith was then being preached in the church. To prove that "righteousness by faith" was being taught by Adventists, Froom indiscriminately cited nearly everyone who used the term. He was either a careless scholar or he could not distinguish between Catholic and Protestant justification. But Froom had good company. He said:

> A. G. Daniells, in a sermon in the Battle Creek Tabernacle at the General Conference of 1901, referred to the powerful effects of another series of Waggoner sermons on Righteousness by Faith at the 1891 Conference. He said: "Do you know that the mighty pulsations of your meeting here in this Tabernacle were felt all around the

---

17. Waggoner, *Confession of Faith*, pp. 14-15.

> globe? We felt them in Australia, and when we got the [1891] *Bulletins*, and began to read, our hearts were stirred, and I have seen our brethren sit and read those messages with the tears streaming down their cheeks; I have seen them fairly convulsed with the power there was in the message, even though only printed in the *Bulletin*; I felt it myself."[18]

Other areas in Waggoner's thought combined with his ideas on righteousness by faith to form his transitional theology of 1889-1891.

The Divinity of Christ

From March 25 to April 22, 1889, Waggoner wrote four articles for the *Signs* on the divinity of Christ. Much of this material was incorporated into his book, *Christ and His Righteousness*, in 1890. Waggoner tried to boldly confess Christ's divinity. He denied that Christ is a created being. He said that Christ is God, both Creator and Lawgiver. These views were more advanced than the blatant Arianism of such early Seventh-day Adventists as Uriah Smith, who declared that Christ was created.

Nevertheless, Waggoner was still Arian in the classical sense. He taught that the Father existed before the Son and that the personality of the Son had a beginning.

> In arguing the perfect equality of the Father and the Son, and the fact that Christ is in very nature God, we do not design to be understood as teaching that the Father was not before the Son. It should not be necessary to guard this point, lest some should think that the Son existed as soon as the Father; yet some go to that extreme, which adds nothing to the dignity of Christ, but rather

18. LeRoy E. Froom, *Movement of Destiny*, p. 263.

> detracts from the honor due him, since many throw the whole thing away rather than accept a theory so obviously out of harmony with the language of Scripture, that Jesus is the *only begotten Son* of God. He was begotten, not created. He is of the substance of the Father, so that in his very nature he is God; and since this is so, "it pleased the Father that in him should all fullness dwell." Col. 1:19.
>
> Some have difficulty in reconciling Christ's statement in John 14:28, "My Father is greater than I," with the idea that he is God, and is entitled to worship. Some, indeed, dwell upon that text alone as sufficient to overthrow the idea of Christ's divinity, but if that were allowed, it would only prove a contradiction in the Bible, and even in Christ's own speech, for it is most positively declared, as well as seen, that he is divine. There are two facts which are amply sufficient to account for Christ's statement recorded in John 14:28. One is that Christ is the Son of God. While both are of the same nature, the Father is first in point of time. He is the greater in that he had no beginning, while Christ's personality had a beginning.[19]

There is no evidence, however, that this misunderstanding of Christ's full divinity contributed to Waggoner's developing pantheism. His views in this area were more advanced than much Seventh-day Adventism of his time. In this respect Waggoner was moving toward a more exalted view of Jesus Christ. It was sorely needed. But Froom's theory that 1888 served to correct Adventism on such eternal verities as the Trinity and the deity of Christ is unsupported by the evidence. Correction in these areas seems to have come more from the writings of Ellen G. White after 1888 than from the contributions of Waggoner and Jones.

---

19. E. J. Waggoner, "The Divinity of Christ" (cont.), *Signs of the Times*, 8 Apr. 1889, p. 214.

The Humanity of Christ

There is no evidence that Waggoner's teaching on the humanity of Christ was part of his message in 1888. This is one of the Waggoner myths demolished by an investigation of the original sources.

However, in the 1889-1891 period Waggoner began giving great prominence to the humanity of Christ. He argued mainly from Romans 8:3 and Hebrews 2:14-17 that the human nature or "flesh" of Christ was sinful and under the condemnation of the law like the rest of mankind (Gal. 4:4, 5). According to Waggoner, Christ's human nature inherited all the tendencies of sin and sinful passions common to all men. Waggoner said:

> A little thought will be sufficient to show anybody that if Christ took upon himself the likeness of man, in order that he might suffer death, it must have been sinful man that he was made like, for it is only sin that causes death. Death could have no power over a sinless man, as Adam was in Eden; and it could not have had any power over Christ if the Lord had not laid on him the iniquity of us all. Moreover, the fact that Christ took upon himself the flesh, not of a sinless being, but of sinful man, that is, that the flesh which he assumed had all the weaknesses and sinful tendencies to which fallen human nature is subject, is shown by the very words upon which this article is based. He was "made of the seed of David according to the flesh." David had all the passions of human nature. He says of himself, "Behold, I was shapen in iniquity; and in sin did my mother conceive me." Ps. 51:5.
>
> A brief glance at the ancestry and posterity of David will show that the line from which Christ sprang, as to his human nature, was such as would tend to concentrate in him all the weaknesses of humanity. To go back to Jacob, we find that before he was converted he had a most unlovely disposition, selfish, crafty, deceitful. His sons partook of the same nature, and Pharez, one of the ancestors of Christ (Matt. 1:3; Gen. 38), was born of a

harlot. Rahab, an unenlightened heathen, became an ancestor of Christ. The weakness and idolatry of Solomon are proverbial. Of Rehoboam, Abijah, Jehoram, Ahaz, Manasseh, Amon, and, other kings of Judah, the record is about the same. They sinned and made the people sin. Some of them had not one redeeming trait in their characters, being worse than the heathen around them. It was from such an ancestry that Christ came. Although his mother was a pure and godly woman, as could but be expected, no one can doubt that the human nature of Christ must have been more subject to the infirmities of the flesh than it would have been if he had been born before the race had so greatly deteriorated physically and morally. This was not accidental, but was a necessary part of the great plan of human redemption, as the following will show:—

"For verily he took not on him the nature of angels; but he took on him the seed of Abraham. [The Syriac version has it, "For he did not assume a nature from angels, but he assumed a nature from the seed of Abraham."] Wherefore in all things it behooved him to be made like unto his brethren, that he might be a merciful and faithful high priest in things pertaining to God, to make reconciliation for the sins of the people. For in that he himself hath suffered being tempted, he is able to succor them that are tempted." Heb. 2:16-18.

If he was made in all things like unto his brethren, then he must have suffered all the infirmities and passions of his brethren. Only so could he be able to help them. So he had to become man, not only that he might die, but that he might be able to sympathize with and succor those who suffer the fierce temptations which Satan brings through the weakness of the flesh. Two more texts that put this matter very forcibly will be sufficient evidence on this point. We quote first 2 Cor. 5:21:—

"For he [God] hath made him [Christ] to be sin for us, who knew no sin; that we might be made the righteousness of God in him."

This is much stronger than the statement that he was made "in the likeness of sinful flesh." He was *made to be sin.* Here is a greater mystery than that the Son of God should die. The spotless Lamb of God, who knew no sin,

> was made to be sin. Sinless, yet not only counted as a sinner, but actually taking upon himself sinful nature. He was made to be sin in order that we might be made righteousness. So Paul to the Galatians says that "God sent forth his Son, made of a woman, made under the law, to redeem them that were under the law, that we might receive the adoption of sons." Gal. 4:4, 5.
>
> That Christ should be born under the law was a necessary consequence of his being born of a woman, taking on him the nature of Abraham, being made of the seed of David, in the likeness of sinful flesh. Human nature is sinful, and the law of God condemns all sin. Not that men are born into the world directly condemned by the law, for in infancy they have no knowledge of right and wrong and are incapable of doing either, but they are born with sinful tendencies, owing to the sins of their ancestors. And when Christ came into the world, he came subject to all the conditions to which other children are subject. . . .
>
> His humanity only veiled his divine nature, which was more than able to successfully resist the sinful passions of the flesh. There was in his whole life a struggle. The flesh, moved upon by the enemy of all righteousness, would tend to sin, yet his divine nature never for a moment harbored an evil desire, nor did his divine power for a moment waver. Having suffered in the flesh all that all men can possibly suffer, he returned to the throne of the Father, as spotless as when he left the courts of glory.[20]

> The human nature that he took was a sinful nature, one subject to sin. If it were not, he would not be a perfect Saviour.[21]

Waggoner's error on the humanity of Christ was not his stress on Christ's union with the fallen race. This is a great truth that needs to be emphasized. The best teach-

---

20. E. J. Waggoner, "God Manifest in the Flesh," *Signs of the Times*, 21 Jan. 1889, p. 39.

21. E. J. Waggoner, "Christ, the Sinless One," *Signs of the Times*, 9 June 1890, p. 342.

ers of the Christian church have always taught that Christ partook of the substance of human nature and assumed all the "essential properties" of human nature. Moreover, they confessed that He assumed the infirmities of human nature resulting from the Fall.

But in stressing Christ's union with the race, Waggoner failed to maintain any distinction between that humanity conceived by the Holy Spirit in the womb of the virgin and the rest of humanity conceived in sin by two earthly parents (Ps. 51:5). The orthodox Christian faith confesses that Christ took all the "essential properties" of human nature even as they had been affected by the Fall. It also confesses that sin—sinfulness, sinful passions, sinful tendencies or original sin—is not an "essential property" of human nature. Like Adam before the Fall, Christ was truly human because sin was no part of His human nature. If He had possessed a sinful nature like the rest of us, He would have been less than truly human. The true church of all ages has confessed that Christ became like us in all things, sin only excepted (Heb. 4:15). But Waggoner failed to make that distinction.[22]

---

22. Some have seen a similarity in the writings of E. J. Waggoner and Ellen G. White on the human nature of Christ. It is true that Mrs. White stressed Christ's union with the fallen race. But Mrs. White did what Waggoner failed to do—she stressed at the same time the distinction between Christ's human nature and the human nature common to the rest of humanity. A sample of these distinction statements are as follows:

"He was born without a taint of sin" (Letter 97, 1898; cited in *Seventh-day Adventists Answer Questions on Doctrine*, p. 657).

"He is a brother in our infirmities, but not in possessing like passions. As the sinless One, His nature recoiled from evil" (Ellen G. White, *Testimonies for the Church*, 2:202; statement appeared in 1869).

"We should have no misgivings in regard to the perfect sinlessness of the human nature of Christ. . . . This holy Substitute is able to save to the uttermost" (*Signs of the Times*, 9 June 1898; cited in Ellen G. White, *Selected Messages*, 1:256).

"Be careful, exceedingly careful as to how you dwell upon the human nature

Waggoner misused two scriptures—Galatians 4:4 and 2 Corinthians 5:21. Christ was under the condemnation of the law only because our sins were imputed to Him, not because our sinful nature was imparted to Him. Christ was "made to be sin for us," not by giving Him a sinful human nature, but as the context shows, by imputing to Him the sins of the world.

Waggoner apparently abandoned the biblical concept of imputation with respect to both Christ and the believer. In the biblical concept Christ was condemned because our sin was imputed to Him, and we are justified because His righteousness is imputed to us. Waggoner was at least consistent within his own framework. But by 1891 he had apparently abandoned the forensic categories of biblical thought. His developing idea of the unity—without distinction—of Christ's human nature with all men played a significant role in his developing pantheism after 1891. He later repeatedly appealed to this view of the incarnation to support his pantheism.

Waggoner did not enunciate a new heresy in his unfortunate theological development. In church history many have followed the same path. Louis Berkhof and Augustus Strong have shown that the doctrine of the sinful nature of Christ logically leads to the abandonment of justification by an imputed righteousness on the one hand and to the development of pantheism on the other.[23]

---

of Christ. Do not set Him before the people as a man with the propensities of sin. . . . Not for one moment was there in Him an evil propensity" (Ellen G. White, Letter 8, 1895; cited in *The Seventh-day Adventist Bible Commentary*, 5:1128).

23. "It knows of no justification, and conceives of salvation as consisting in subjective sanctification" (Louis Berkhof, *Systematic Theology*, p. 390).

"In . . . [this] theory there is no imputation, or representation, or substitution. . . .

Of course, some who hold a theory of the sinful human nature of Christ do not discard imputed righteousness and do not embrace pantheism. This is because they do not follow their Christology to its logical conclusion. But Waggoner seemed to be both blessed and cursed. He possessed a logical mind that followed every premise to its natural and inevitable end.

The Atonement

Toward the close of 1890 Waggoner presented a mystical view of the atonement which later played a fateful role in his developing pantheism.[24] His view of the atonement was the result of repudiating forensic justification for an "effective" justification. Simply stated, Waggoner's theory was that the blood of Christ is the life of Christ. In death Christ gave us His life. Mystically poured into us, this life accomplishes our forgiveness and justification.

This enticing theory in effect denies the legal penalty for sin that was paid on the cross. The death of Christ is simply regarded as a means of pouring out His life so that it can be poured into us. God pardons by inner renewal. He forgives by healing the disease. And He justifies by sanctifying.

Waggoner's view on the blood of Christ was not new to Christian theology.[25] It was popularized in the nine-

---

"It necessitates the surrender of the doctrine of justification as a merely declaratory act of God; and requires such a view of the divine holiness, expressed only through the order of nature, as can be maintained only upon principles of pantheism" (Augustus H. Strong, *Systematic Theology*, pp. 746-47).

24. Waggoner, *Power of Forgiveness*, pp. 5-6.

25. "Theories which conceive the work of Christ as *terminating physically on man*, so affecting him as to bring him by an interior and hidden working upon

him into participation with the one life of Christ; the so-called 'mystical theories.' The fundamental characteristic of these theories is their discovery of the saving fact not in anything which Christ taught or did, but in what he was. It is upon the Incarnation, rather than upon Christ's teaching or his work that they throw stress, attributing the saving power of Christ not to what he does for us but to what he does in us. Tendencies to this type of theory are already traceable in the Platonizing Fathers; and with the entrance of the more developed Neoplatonism into the stream of Christian thinking, through the writings of the Pseudo-Dionysius naturalized in the West by Johannes Scotus Erigena, a constant tradition of mystical teaching began which never died out. In the Reformation age this type of thought was represented by men like Osiander, Schwenckfeld, Franck, Weigel, Boehme. In the modern Church a new impulse was given to essentially the same mode of conception by Schleiermacher and his followers (e.g., C. I. Nitzsch, Rothe, Schoberlein, Lange, Martensen), among whom what is known as the 'Mercersburg School' . . . will be particularly interesting to Americans (e.g., J. W. Nevin, *The Mystical Presence*, Philadelphia, 1846). A very influential writer among English theologians of the same general class was F. D. Maurice (1805-72), although he added to his fundamental mystical conception of the work of Christ the further notions that Christ fully identified himself with us and, thus partaking of our sufferings, set us a perfect example of sacrifice of self to God (cf. especially *Theological Essays*, London, 1853; *The Doctrine of Sacrifice*, Cambridge, 1854; new ed., 1879). Here, too, must be classed the theory suggested in the writings of the late B. F. Westcott (*The Victory of the Cross*, London, 1888), which was based on a hypothesis of the efficacy of Christ's blood, borrowed apparently directly from William Milligan (cf. *The Ascension and Heavenly Highpriesthood of our Lord*, London, 1892) though it goes back ultimately to the Socinians, to the effect that Christ's offering of himself is not to be identified with his sufferings and death, but rather with the presentation of his life (which is in his blood, set free by death for this purpose) in heaven. 'Taking this blood as efficacious by virtue of the vitality which it contains, Dr. Westcott holds that it was set free from Christ's body that it might vitalize ours, as it were, by transfusion' (C. H. Waller, in the *Presbyterian and Reformed Review*, ii, 1892, p. 656). Somewhat similarly H. Clay Trumbell (*The Blood Covenant*, New York, 1885) looks upon sacrifices as only a form of blood covenanting, i.e., of instituting blood-brotherhood between man and God by transfusion of blood; and explains the sacrifice of Christ as representing communing in blood, i.e., in the principle of life, between God and man, both of whom Christ represents. The theory which has been called 'salvation by sample,' or salvation 'by gradually extirpated depravity,' also has its affinities here. Something like it is as old as Felix of Urgel (d. 818 . . .), and it has been taught in its full development by Dippel (1673-1734), Swedenborg (1688-1772), Menken (1768-1831), and especially by Edward Irving (1792-1834), and, of course, by the modern followers of Swedenborg (e.g., B. F. Barrett). The essence of this theory is that what was assumed by our Lord was human nature as he found it, that is, as fallen; and that this human nature, as assumed by him, was by the power of his divine nature (or of the Holy Spirit dwelling in him beyond measure) not only kept from sinning, but purified from sin and presented perfect before God as the first-fruits of a saved humanity; men being saved as they become partakers (by faith) of this purified humanity, as they become leavened by

teenth century by Bishop B. F. Westcott in *The Victory of the Cross*.[26] Westcott argued that in shedding His blood, Christ gave His life to all men. Westcott's concept that the life is in the blood was based on Leviticus 17:10. In death Christ surrendered His life and made it available to men.[27]

Waggoner's developing theory of the mystical atonement is of particular interest because of its connection with pantheism. In his *Reformed Dogmatics* Herman Hoeksema says, "Many of the mystical theologians are either pantheistic or have a strong pantheistic tendency."[28]

Historical theology also shows that the mystical theory of atonement stresses the incarnation more than the cross and is therefore often found in association with the doctrine of the sinful human nature of Christ. Waggoner apparently imbibed some of these theories from his wide reading, especially after going to England in 1892.

---

this new leaven. Certain of the elements which the great German theologian J. C. K. von Hofmann built into his complicated and not altogether stable theory—a theory which was the occasion of much discussion about the middle of the nineteenth century—reproduce some of the characteristic language of the theory of 'salvation by sample'" (*The New Schaff-Herzog Encyclopedia of Religious Knowledge*, 1:351-52).

26. A series of six sermons preached by Bishop B. F. Westcott during Holy Week in 1888 and afterwards (London, 1888), published under the title, *The Victory of the Cross*. For a summary of Westcott's mystical theory of the atonement, see T. H. Hughes, *The Atonement: Modern Theories of the Doctrine*, pp. 243-50.

27. The mistaken idea that blood means life is effectively refuted in modern times by A. M. Stibbs, *The Meaning of the Word 'Blood' in Scripture*, and Leon Morris, *The Apostolic Preaching of the Cross*, pp. 112-28.

28. Herman Hoeksema, *Reformed Dogmatics*, p. 388. Cf. Loraine Boettner's statement:

"The mystical theory is essentially pantheistic in its tendency. Its assertion that divine life was infused into the human in order to purify and lift the human to the divine breaks down the fundamental distinction between God and man, and leaves the way open for a pantheistic interpretation of life" (Loraine Boettner, *Studies in Theology*, p. 347).

Sanctification

The righteousness of faith is Christ's righteousness alone. The righteousness which is by faith alone was done without the believer's work or activity. As long as we recognize that we are justified by a righteousness in which we had no share, a righteousness which is by faith alone, we are on solid ground. But if we confound sanctification with righteousness by faith, we are involved in serious heresy. Confounding righteousness by faith and sanctification was fatal for Waggoner's theory of sanctification.

The best Protestant authors have never taught that sanctification is part of righteousness by faith. They have never taught that sanctification is by faith alone.[29] Man is both a creature and a person. Because he is a

---

29. J. C. Ryle writes:

"As to the phrase 'holiness by faith,' I find it nowhere in the New Testament. Without controversy, in the matter of our justification before God, faith in Christ is the one thing needful. All that simply believe are justified. Righteousness is imputed 'to him that worketh not but believeth.' (Rom. iv. 5.) It is thoroughly Scriptural and right to say 'faith alone justifies.' But it is not equally Scriptural and right to say 'faith alone sanctifies.' The saying requires very large qualification. Let one fact suffice. We are frequently told that a man is 'justified by faith without the deeds of the law,' by St. Paul. But not once are we told that we are 'sanctified by faith without the deeds of the law.' On the contrary, we are expressly told by St. James that the faith whereby we are *visibly and demonstratively* justified before man, is a faith which 'if it hath not works is dead, being alone.' (James ii. 17.) I may be told, in reply, that no one of course means to disparage 'works' as an essential part of a holy life. It would be well, however, to make this more plain than many seem to make it in these days.

" . . . I ask, in the second place, whether it is wise to make so little as some appear to do, comparatively, of the many *practical exhortations to holiness in daily life* which are to be found in the Sermon on the Mount, and in the latter part of most of St. Paul's epistles? Is it according to the proportion of God's Word? I doubt it" (J. C. Ryle, *Holiness*, p. ix).

Cf. J. M. Cramp: "True Protestants never maintained the absurd position, that we are sanctified by faith only" (J. M. Cramp, *The Council of Trent*, p. 54).

creature, God must sanctify him. In that sense a holy life is a gift of God. But because man is also a person, he must cooperate with God in living a holy life. He is called to work, strive, wrestle, run and fight. There is to be meaningful human activity. God gives the power. Man obeys and forms a character. God does not propose to use him like a robot, to do the believing and obeying for him. The work for him was a substitutionary work done by the Mediator.

It may sound pious and superspiritual to say Christ lives the victorious life in the believer. But this fails to do justice to both the Old and New Testament, which ascribe the work of faith to the believer. The Bible does not hesitate to speak of "your righteousness" (Deut. 6:25), "his [the believer's] righteousness" (Ezek. 33:18), "your work of faith" and "labour of love" (1 Thess. 1:3) and "good works" (1 Tim. 6:18). The works of the believer are *his* works—even though they may be the result of the Spirit's thrust in his life. And the believer will be judged by his works. If they were only the works God did in and through him, the believer's personality would be lost in union with the divine. The distinction between the work of the Creator and the work of the believer would also be lost. This must logically lead to perfectionism—for is not God's work powerful? And it must logically lead to pantheism.

Unfortunately, between 1889 and 1891 Waggoner moved in this direction with his extreme views of sanctification. These views could have been avoided if he had preserved the distinction between righteousness by faith alone and sanctification. On February 4, 1889, he made the incredible statement that the obedience of the Christian "is not his personal action."[30] If sanctified obe-

---

30. Waggoner, "Obedience of Faith," p. 71.

dience were the righteousness of faith, what other conclusion could he logically draw?

In his lectures on Romans in 1891, Waggoner said:

> "It is God which worketh in you both to will and to do of his good pleasure." We give ourselves into the hands of Christ. He comes and *takes up his abode* with us. We are as clay in the hands of the potter; but it is Christ who does all the good works, and to him belongs all the glory.[31]
>
> His obedience must be manifested in us day by day. It is not our obedience, but the obedience of Christ working in us.[32]

These statements would be innocent aberrations if not taken too seriously or pressed too far. Similar statements are found in the teaching and writing of many pious believers. They sound like humble and spiritual confessions of dependence on Christ's grace. And if that is all that is meant, we should place the best construction upon them. But Waggoner relentlessly pressed these premises until they bore fruit in the most outrageous perfectionism and pantheism. Waggoner's developing theology should be a warning to us. For all the features of his 1889-1891 thought are with us today in the current Adventist struggle over righteousness by faith.

The Righteousness of God

Waggoner often wrote about the relationship between the righteousness of God and the law of God. Beginning with his first writings in 1884, he correctly declared that

---

31. Waggoner, *Book of Romans*, p. 7.
32. Ibid., p. 15.

the law of God is an expression of the righteousness of God. But in the years between 1889 and 1891 Waggoner seemed to stress this point until he appeared to say that the law is an exhaustive expression of the righteousness of God. In "Living by Faith" he declared that "the righteousness of God is the perfect law."[33] This is like turning the biblical statements "God is love" and "God is light" into "love is God" and "light is God." Love, light and law are aspects of God's character. But it cannot be said that any one is an exhaustive expression of God. In the same way, law is not an exhaustive expression of God's righteousness (Rom. 1:16, 17).

If law were an exhaustive expression of God's righteousness, as Waggoner seems to imply, then law and gospel would be indistinguishable. Waggoner had not come quite that far in 1891. But we shall see that he drew the inevitable conclusions in 1894.

Summary

Waggoner's theology between 1889 and 1891 was a theology in transition. Although not at first abandoning forensic justification, he moved to a concept of "effective" justification. And effective justification soon eclipsed forensic justification altogether. Along with the Roman Catholic concept of effective justification, Waggoner developed such supportive concepts as the sinful human nature of Christ, the mystical atonement, sanctification by faith alone, and the law as an exhaustive expression of God's righteousness.

Both church history and the history of theology clearly demonstrate that these are pantheistic premises.

---

33. E. J. Waggoner, "Living by Faith," *Signs of the Times*, 25 Mar. 1889, p. 182. Cf. idem, *Christ and His Righteousness*, pp. 47-8.

Waggoner's theology became subjective and internalistic. His own *Confession* shows that as early as 1891 he saw no value in the intercessory ministry of the High Priest in the heavenly service. He had departed from the concept of salvation by imputation, substitution and representation. Grace was wholly confined within the believer. Waggoner lost the anchor outside himself, the anchor that enters "within the veil." His theology was a theology of immanence which lost sight of the transcendent God.

Waggoner rose no higher than he did at the conference of 1888. It would be unwise, even dangerous, to look for the 1888 message in his writings after that time.

8

Waggoner in Decline: 1892-1897

One feature characterizes Waggoner's theological decline after he became editor of the British *Present Truth* in 1892. In almost every area *his theology blurred essential distinctions.*

All sound theology must have both union and distinction. In this respect theology must be like music. Without a distinction of notes, there is no music. And without a harmony of notes, there is no music. Let us consider some theological illustrations.

The Christian religion is Trinitarian. We must distinguish the persons of the Trinity. The Father sent the Son, the Son died on the cross, and the Spirit incorporates us into Christ's holy history. We must distinguish between the work of the Mediator—the High-Priestly intercession of blood—and the Holy Spirit's work in the heart. The first is substitutionary; the second is not. On the other hand, we must maintain the essential unity of the persons of the Godhead. Where One is present, God is present. Only in this way can we hold the transcendence of God and the immanence of

God in proper tension.

The same principle is true in Christology. We must distinguish the divine and the human nature of Christ. We must be careful not to confound them. And we must confess their union in the one person of Christ.

Soteriology illustrates the same point. Justification must be distinguished from sanctification. There must be no fusion. But justification must also exist in inseparable union with sanctification. There must be no separation. A sound theology must have union without fusion, distinction without separation. This principle applies to every important area of Christian thought.

The Western mind has sometimes been tempted to lose the union while holding to the distinction. This has happened in anthropology, where the wholistic concept of man has been lost. Scholastic Protestantism stressed the distinction between the law and the gospel in such a way that it lost a true sense of their union. This emphasis on distinction without a corresponding emphasis on union tended toward Deism. Religion became abstract, dry and sterile.

Just as a loss of union leads to Deism, which stresses only the transcendence of God, so the loss of distinction leads to pantheism, which stresses only the immanence of God. Deism has been the tendency of the Western mind. Pantheism is the tendency of the Eastern mind. In their concept of the creature's union with the Deity, the great Eastern religions have lost the distinction between the Creator and the creature.

Waggoner lost the essential element of distinction in his theology. Indeed, in most areas he explicitly denied any distinction.

1. He lost the distinction between justification and sanctification, the righteousness of faith and the righteousness of the law.

2. He lost the distinction between the law and the gospel.

3. He lost the distinction between the human nature of Christ and the human nature of all other men.

4. He lost the distinction between Christ's work for us on the cross and His work in our hearts.

5. He lost the distinction between believer and unbeliever.

6. He lost the distinction between physical light and spiritual light, physical water and spiritual water, air and the Holy Spirit.

7. He lost the distinction between heaven as God's dwelling place and the believer's heart as God's dwelling place.

8. He lost the distinction between the temple of God in heaven and the temple of the church and the believer on earth.

9. He lost the distinction between ordinary food and drink and the actual body and blood of Christ.

10. He lost the distinction between his relationship to his own wife and another woman.

These are all aspects of one fundamental error. Waggoner lost the proper distinction between the Creator and the creature. His theology became pantheistic. We will now document Waggoner's loss of all vital theological distinctions.

On Justification

Waggoner's understanding of justification by faith was central to his theology. Luther had declared that justification by faith is the article of the standing or falling church. It was certainly the loss of this article that caused Waggoner's fall.

From 1892 to 1896 a veritable torrent of articles flowed from Waggoner's pen as editor of the British *Present Truth.* He repeatedly affirmed his theory of an effective justification. He completely confounded justification with sanctification. And he openly repudiated the concept of imputed righteousness—denying that the righteousness lived out historically by Christ is reckoned to the believing sinner. Waggoner argued that the actual life of Christ is infused into the sinner and that this infused life justifies or makes him effectively righteous.

In his view of justification Waggoner was one with the Roman Catholics, the Quakers and many mystic Anabaptists. To him the believer is not justified because Christ lived a righteous life for him historically and died on the cross historically. Rather, the believer is justified because Christ's living in his heart has actually made him conformable to the law. Likewise, forgiveness of sins does not come to the believer because Christ paid the penalty for them on the cross. Rather, the life of Christ in the believer has actually erased the sinfulness and replaced it with His indwelling life. Waggoner repeatedly expressed this theme.

In his article, "Saved by His Life," Waggoner said:

> When Christ gives Himself to a man, He gives the whole of His life. Each individual who believes gets the whole of Christ. He gets His life as an infant, as a child, as a youth, and as a mature man. The man who acknowleges that his whole life has been nothing but sin, and who willingly gives it up for Christ's life, makes a complete exchange, and has Christ's life from infancy up to manhood, in the place of his own. So he must necessarily be counted just before God. He is justified, not because God has con-

> sented to ignore his sin because of his faith, but because God has made him a righteous man—a doer of the law—by giving him His own righteous life.
>
> That the forgiveness of sins is by receiving the life of Christ in the place of the sinful life, is shown by the statement concerning Christ, that "we have redemption through His blood, even the forgiveness of sins." Col. i. 14. "It is the blood that maketh an atonement for the soul," "for the life of the flesh is in the blood." Lev. xvii. 11. So we have redemption through the blood of Christ, are reconciled to God by His death, because in His death He gives us His life.
>
> The receiving of that life by faith makes us stand before God as though we had never sinned. The law scrutinizes us, and can find nothing wrong, because our old life is gone, and the life that we now have—the life of Christ—has never done anything wrong.[1]

In his article entitled "Being Justified" Waggoner defined the term *justification* as follows:

> Justification has to do with the law. The term means making just. Now in Romans ii. 13 we are told who the just ones are. "For not the hearers of the law are just before God, but the doers of the law shall be justified." The just man, therefore, is the one who does the law. To be just means to be righteous. Therefore since the just man is the one who does the law, it follows that to justify a man, that is, to make him just, is to make him a doer of the law.[2]

In the same article Waggoner echoed John Henry Newman, who had suggested that when God declares a

---

1. E. J. Waggoner, "Saved by His Life," *Present Truth*, 6 Oct. 1892, p. 308.
2. E. J. Waggoner, "Being Justified," *Present Truth*, 20 Oct. 1892, pp. 323-24.

sinner righteous, His very word makes him righteous.[3] Newman incorrectly used the argument of the Genesis creation epic: When God said, "Let there be light," immediately there was light. So Waggoner said:

> God justifies the ungodly. Is that not right? Certainly it is. It does not mean that he glosses over a man's faults, so that he is counted righteous, although he is really wicked; but it means that He makes that man a doer of the law. We have the fact considered in another part of this paper, that when God speaks a thing, that moment that thing is so. The moment God declares an ungodly man righteous, that instant that man is a doer of the law. Surely that is a good work, and a just work, as well as a merciful one.
>
> How is the man justified, or made righteous? "Being justified freely by His grace, through the redemption that is in Christ Jesus." Rom. iii. 24. Remember that to justify means to make one a doer of the law, and then read the passage again. "Being made a doer of the law freely, through the redemption that is in Christ Jesus." The redemption that is in Christ Jesus is the worthiness or the purchasing power of Christ. He gives Himself to the sinner; His righteousness is given to the one who has

3. John Henry Newman began as an Anglican, became a leading figure in the high-church Oxford Movement of the 1830's, turned Roman Catholic and ended as a cardinal. His *Lectures on Justification* was published in 1838 when he was an Anglican and republished, with the addition of corrective notations, in 1874 after his conversion to Roman Catholicism.

sinned, and who believes.[4]

Waggoner denied the historic Protestant and Pauline concept of imputed righteousness.

> That does not mean that Christ's righteousness which He did eighteen hundred years ago is laid up for the sinner, to be simply credited to his account, but it means that His present, active righteousness is given to that man. Christ comes to live in that man who believes, for He dwells in the heart by faith. So the man who was a sinner is transformed into a new man, having the very righteousness of God.[5]

This statement appears to be Waggoner's first open denial of the imputation of the life of Christ lived as Jesus of Nazareth. Waggoner repeated this significant denial more strongly in subsequent years. For example, he said:

---

4. Waggoner, "Being Justified," p. 324. Newman's argument was often repeated by Waggoner. Cf. his following statement:

"To declare righteousness is to speak righteousness. God speaks righteousness to man, and then he is righteous. . . .

"The justice of declaring a sinner to be righteous lies in the fact that he is actually made righteous. Whatever God declares to be so, is so. And then he is made righteous by the life of God given him in Christ. The sin is against God, and if He is willing to forgive it, He has the right to do so. No unbeliever would deny the right of a man to overlook a trespass against him. But God does not simply overlook the trespass; He gives His life as a forfeit. Thus He upholds the majesty of the law, and is just in declaring that man righteous, who was before a sinner. Sin is remitted—sent away—from the sinner, because sin and righteousness cannot exist together, and God puts His own righteous life into the believer. So God is merciful in His justice, and just in His mercy" (E. J. Waggoner, "Studies in Romans: The Justice of Mercy," *Present Truth*, 30 Aug. 1894, pp. 548-50).

It should be noted how Waggoner drastically alters the meaning of Romans 3:26. In context Paul means that God is shown to be just in justifying the believing sinner because Christ died for him (Rom. 3:25). But Waggoner says that God is just in declaring the believing sinner righteous because He makes him righteous. Waggoner transfers the ground of justification from the cross to the sanctification of the believer.

5. Waggoner, "Being Justified," p. 324.

> It is not that we are counted righteous because Jesus of Nazareth was righteous eighteen hundred years ago, but because "He ever liveth," "the same yesterday, and to-day, and for ever," to save by the power of His endless life, all that come to Him.[6]

On September 21, 1893, Waggoner expounded his view of effective justification—confounding justification and sanctification. He taught that we are forgiven by being healed through the infusion of Christ's life. This theory was directly linked to his mystical theory of the atonement. Waggoner declared: "Being made partakers of the life of God, through faith in Christ's death, we are at peace with Him, because one life is in us both. Then we are 'saved by His life.'"[7]

The apostle Paul teaches we have peace with God because Christ at the right hand of God is our peace and His perfect righteousness is reckoned as ours (Rom. 5:1; Eph. 2:15). Or again, we have peace with God *because* of the blood of the cross. The word *because* is very important in the doctrine of salvation. It indicates the ground of our justification and peace. Waggoner's "because" in his statement above indicates that he believed the ground of peace is Christ's indwelling life—our sanctification. Waggoner internalized everything. Instead of justification on the ground of Christ's work done for us, he had justification on the ground of the work of Christ's Spirit in us.

---

6. E. J. Waggoner, "A Lesson from Real Life," *Present Truth*, 31 May 1894, pp. 338-39. Cf. "The Bible does not teach us that God calls us righteous simply because Jesus of Nazareth was righteous eighteen hundred years ago. It says that by His obedience *we are made righteous*. Notice that it is present, actual righteousness" (E. J. Waggoner, "Studies in Romans: The Free Gift," *Present Truth*, 18 Oct. 1894, p. 660).

7. E. J. Waggoner, "Why Did Christ Die?" *Present Truth*, 21 Sept. 1893, p. 388.

On July 26, 1894, Waggoner repeated his view of effective or Roman Catholic justification: "Let it not be forgotten that 'just' means 'righteous,' and that both mean a state of harmony with the law of God, which is *his* life."[8] Again, on August 30 of the same year, he wrote: " 'Being Justified.'—In other words, being made righteous. To justify means to make righteous. God supplies just what the sinner lacks. Let no reader forget the simple meaning of justification."[9] Then, on October 18, he wrote:

> Men are not simply counted righteous, but actually *made righteous*, by the obedience of Christ, who is as righteous as He ever was, and who lives to-day in those who yield to Him. His ability to live in any human being is shown by the fact that He took human flesh eighteen hundred years ago. What God did in the person of the carpenter of Nazareth, He is willing and anxious to do for every man that now lives.[10]

During 1895 Waggoner did not appear to substantially modify his doctrine of justification. On April 23, 1896, he made the following interesting statement:

> A friend has forwarded to me a severe condemnation of a statement made some time ago, to the effect that *to justify* means *to make righteous*. . . . It was stated [by me] that "being justified" means "being made righteous," because that definition is patent from the reading of the English Bible.[11]

Here Waggoner merely reaffirmed his doctrine of 1894.

---

8. E. J. Waggoner, "Studies in Romans: The Law and Judgment," *Present Truth*, 26 July 1894, p. 467.

9. Waggoner, "Justice of Mercy," p. 549.

10. Waggoner, "Free Gift," p. 660.

11. E. J. Waggoner, "The All-Sufficient Life," *Present Truth*, 23 Apr. 1896, p. 259.

On Sanctification

Waggoner spoke of justification or righteousness by faith in terms appropriate only to sanctification. So it is not surprising to find him speaking of sanctification in terms appropriate only to justification. All good Protestant teachers since Luther have regarded justification monergistically—as God's work alone apart from human effort or work of any kind—and sanctification synergistically—as a work which combines divine power and human effort.

Bishop Ryle was typical of any good Protestant when he said:

> As to the phrase "holiness by faith," I find it nowhere in the New Testament. Without controversy, in the matter of our justification before God, faith in Christ is the one thing needful. All that simply believe are justified. Righteousness is imputed "to him that worketh not but believeth." (Rom. iv. 5.) It is thoroughly Scriptural and right to say "faith alone justifies." But it is not equally Scriptural and right to say "faith alone sanctifies." The saying requires very large qualification. Let one fact suffice. We are frequently told that a man is "justified by faith without the deeds of the law," by St. Paul. But not once are we told that we are "sanctified by faith without the deeds of the law." On the contrary, we are expressly told by St. James that the faith whereby we are *visibly and demonstratively* justified before man, is a faith which "if it hath not works is dead, being alone." (James ii. 17.) I may be told, in reply, that no one of course means to disparage "works" as an essential part of a holy life. It would be well, however, to make this more plain than many seem to make it in these days.[12]

---

12. J. C. Ryle, *Holiness*, p. ix.

Bunyan testified:

> If you do not put a difference between justification wrought by the Man Christ without, and sanctification wrought by the Spirit of Christ within . . . you are not able to divide the word aright; but contrariwise, you corrupt the word of God, and cast stumbling-blocks before the people, and will certainly one day most deeply smart for your folly, except you repent.[13]

As early as 1889 Waggoner began to lose this important distinction between justification and sanctification. Between 1892 and 1894, and especially in 1894, he wrote about the believer's holy life as if it were God's work alone. He applied substitutionary language to the work of the indwelling Christ in the believer's heart. He said that it is not the believer who believes or obeys. It is God Himself who does it for—instead of—the believer. Waggoner had the mystic's view of the union of the soul with God in which the individuality and personality of the soul disappear and God is represented as doing everything in the believer.

On July 14, 1892, Waggoner said:

> Henceforth, then, it is to be the life of Christ that meets the temptations of Satan, and labours to do the Father's will. But Jesus Christ is the same yesterday, to-day and forever; therefore the life which is given to us will present the same characteristics that the life of Christ presented when He was on the earth in person; His life in us must be as strong to do and to resist as it was when He lived in Judea.[14]

---

13. John Bunyan, *The Riches of Bunyan*, p. 140.

14. E. J. Waggoner, "Baptism—Its Significance," *Present Truth*, 14 July 1892, p. 217.

If it were Christ who resists temptation and labors to do the Father's will in the believer, then would not this internal righteousness satisfy the law? Apparently Waggoner thought so. This is simply quietism and perfectionism.

Waggoner's view of sanctification was erroneous. Although both faith and a virtuous life are gifts of God's grace, they are at the same time an activity of the believer. They are something he actually and personally does in the freedom of his own individuality. Thus the Bible repeatedly calls such internal righteousness "your righteousness," "his [the believer's] righteousness" and "your good works."

The believer is also an imperfect, mortal vessel still tainted with inbred sinfulness. Because of this he even defiles his prayers, good works, faith, love and whatever he does under the impulse of the Spirit. Thus no righteousness in the believer can satisfy the law. It was sheer heresy for Waggoner to say the believer is forgiven or justified or has peace *because* of this internal righteousness.[15] Martin Chemnitz said that to transfer the cause of justification from the vicarious righteousness of Christ to our renewal or new obedience is blasphemy. If this be so, Waggoner was guilty.

On October 6, 1892, Waggoner wrote:

> And since the only righteous life ever known is the life of God in Christ, it is plain that the sinner must get the life of Christ. This is nothing more nor less than living the Christian life. The Christian life is the life of Christ. . . .

---

15. We need to speak with caution here about Christ's imparted righteousness as if it were as meritorious as imputed righteousness. As far as biblical terminology is concerned, Christ's righteousness refers to His own personal righteousness which is imputed to the believer. The righteous life of the believer is not called Christ's righteousness but the believer's righteousness. We should not try to be more "spiritual" than the Bible.

> Is there no possibility of living the Christian life? Yes, there is, but Christ must be allowed to live it. Men must be content to give up their sinful and worthless lives, and count themselves dead—merely nothing. Then if they are indeed dead with Christ, they will also live with Him. Then it will be with them as it was with Paul: "For I through the law am dead to the law, that I might live unto God. I am crucified with Christ; nevertheless I live; yet not I, but Christ liveth in me; and the life which I now live in the flesh I live by the faith of the Son of God, who loved me, and gave Himself for me." Gal. ii. 19, 20. When Christ is allowed to live His own life in a man, then, and then only, will that man's life be in harmony with the law of God. Then he will have righteousness, because he has the only life in which there is righteousness.[16]

Popular holiness theology is full of this pious-sounding talk. And so is much Seventh-day Adventist literature. An extreme and unbiblical view of sanctification is the fruit of losing the distinction between justification and sanctification. Waggoner's statement above loses the distinction between the life of Christ and the life of the believer. Christ's life is certainly in full harmony with the law. But He is at the right hand of God. The believer's life at its very best still falls short of the glory of God. There is no such thing as a sinless believer (Rom. 3:23; 1 John 1:8).

On October 20, 1892, Waggoner wrote his highly significant article, "Being Justified." It reveals how his conception of justification leads to a corruption of sanctification.

> Faith brings Christ into the heart, and the law of God is in the heart of Christ. And thus "as by one man's disobedience many were made sinners, so by the obedience of

16. E. J. Waggoner, "Righteousness and Life," *Present Truth*, 6 Oct. 1892, p. 308.

> one shall many be made righteous." This one who obeys is the Lord Jesus Christ, and His obedience is done in the heart of every one who believes. And as it is by His obedience alone that men are made doers of the law, so to Him shall be the glory for ever and ever.[17]

It is evident that Waggoner misused Romans 5:19. The text actually refers to the representative obedience of Jesus in contrast to the representative disobedience of Adam. But Waggoner applied the text to an internal righteousness. In the matter of the Christian life he affirmed that the "one who obeys is the Lord Jesus Christ, and His obedience is done in the heart of every one who believes." In contrast, Ellen G. White wrote:

> The Lord does not propose to perform for us either the willing or the doing. This is our proper work. As soon as we earnestly enter upon the work, God's grace is given to work in us to will and to do, but never as a substitute for our effort.[18]

But again, the worst feature of Waggoner's doctrine is that in losing the truth of justification, he lost the distinction that should be preserved between the obedience of Christ and that of the believer.

On March 8, 1894, Waggoner further pressed his extreme view of sanctification.[19] He combined it with his idea that Christ took sinful human flesh. He reasoned that when 1 John 4:2 says, "Jesus Christ is come in the flesh," it means Christ is actually present in all sinful flesh—in everyone in the world. He then went on to say

---

17. Waggoner, "Being Justified," p. 324.

18. Ellen G. White, *Testimonies to Ministers and Gospel Workers*, p. 240.

19. E. J. Waggoner, "Confessing Christ in the Flesh," *Present Truth*, 8 Mar. 1894, pp. 149-53.

that the secret of victory is to confess that Christ is come in the flesh—not historically but existentially. And if we confess what is already true, this Christ in sinful flesh speaks "in us and for us" against the devil. It is "Christ living in us [who] commands him to depart." Waggoner went on to say that Christ will "keep the Sabbath in us" just as He did eighteen hundred years ago.

Again, in "A Lesson from Real Life," Waggoner said: "Christ dwelling in us does the right by His own power. . . . And thus it is that 'by the obedience of one shall many be made righteous.'"[20] Thus Waggoner utterly failed to distinguish between what Christ does for us (Rom. 5:19) and what He does in us.

In his article of October 11, 1894, "Saved by His Life," Waggoner revealed his penchant for internalizing everything. He did not hesitate to use substitutionary language for the indwelling work of Christ—or the Spirit. "We receive," said Waggoner, "His life as a substitute for our sinful life."[21] A careful reading of the context shows he was not discussing Christ's substitutionary life lived in Palestine but Christ's substitutionary life lived in the heart of the believer.

An eminent Protestant theologian once remarked that "nothing can be more unscriptural in itself, or more pernicious to the souls of men, than the substitution of the gracious work of the Spirit *in* us, for the vicarious work of Christ *for* us, as the ground of our pardon and acceptance with God."[22] This is what Waggoner did. Unlike Luther, he failed to distinguish between the cleansing

---

20. Waggoner, "Lesson from Real Life," p. 339.

21. E. J. Waggoner, "Studies in Romans: Saved by His Life," *Present Truth*, 11 Oct. 1894, p. 645.

22. James Buchanan, *The Doctrine of Justification: An Outline of Its History in the Church and of Its Exposition from Scripture*, pp. 387-88.

work of the Mediator —High Priest—which is judicial, instantaneous and by imputation, and the cleansing work of the Holy Spirit, which is experiential and progressive.

On Law and Gospel

We have already noted Waggoner's dangerous tendency to speak of law as if it were the exhaustive expression of the righteousness of God. This tendency bore its fruit. In an article dated July 5, 1894, Waggoner showed that he had lost the distinction between law and gospel and had made them one. Waggoner's mystical wholism made practically everything one—heaven and earth, God and man, physical light and spiritual light. Commenting on the law and the gospel from Romans 1:17, Waggoner said:

> "For therein is the righteousness of God revealed." Wherein?—In the Gospel. Bear in mind that the righteousness of God is His perfect law, a statement of which is found in the ten commandments. There is no such thing as a conflict between the law and the Gospel. Indeed, there are not in reality two such things as the law and the Gospel. The true law of God is the Gospel; for the law is the life of God, and we are "saved by His life." The Gospel reveals the righteous law of God, because the Gospel has the law in itself.[23]

On the Atonement

Waggoner's mystical view of atonement was an integral part of his pantheism. In the period just before

23. E. J. Waggoner, "Studies in Romans: The Righteousness of God," *Present Truth*, 5 July 1894, p. 422.

1891 he adopted Westcott's well-known theory that the blood is life and that Christ died to give us His life. Waggoner, however, carried this theory further than Westcott. He eventually lost sight of Christ's dying in Palestine in A.D. 31 and transposed the historical, objective atonement into something existential and subjective.

Christ, Waggoner said, is crucified and risen in *every man*. This is where and how Christ carries sin. Waggoner's tendency to internalize every great Christian truth was so strong that he dehistoricized the atonement. He made the atonement a mystical, internalistic happening in every man.

Waggoner also rejected the historic Christian doctrine of the substitutionary atonement in which Christ paid the penalty for human sin on the cross. To Waggoner sin was merely a disease of the blood that required healing. There was no objective guilt and therefore no penalty demanded by the divine law. Waggoner said the atonement was never designed to reconcile God to man but only to reconcile man to God. The sacrifice of Christ as a means of propitiating the wrath of God was lampooned as a pagan concept. The biblical concept of God's wrath was altogether dissipated. Waggoner seemed to combine the mystical view of the atonement with what is called "the moral influence theory."

The history of these ideas can be documented in historical theology. Dr. James Buchanan aptly commented that it is almost impossible to invent a new heresy. But since we are here examining Waggoner's history, we shall trace the development of his theory on the atonement.

On October 6, 1892, Waggoner repeated Westcott's theory that the blood means the life of Christ rather than the forfeited life—violent death—of Christ.[24] Waggoner replaced the substitutionary or penal-satisfaction atonement with this concept of the cross.

On September 21, 1893, Waggoner wrote a highly significant article entitled "Why Did Christ Die?" The simple, orthodox Christian explanation that the justice of God requires the penalty of death and that Christ bore this penalty on behalf of the race was wholly absent. Waggoner wrote:

> "But," someone will say, "You have made the reconciliation all on the part of man; I have always been taught that the death of Christ reconciled God to man; that Christ died to satisfy God's justice, and to appease Him." Well, we have left the matter of reconciliation just where the Scriptures have put it: and while they have much to say about the necessity for man to be reconciled to God, they never once hint of such a thing as the necessity for God to be reconciled to man. To intimate the necessity for such a thing is to bring a grave charge against the character of God. The idea has come into the Christian Church from the Papacy, which in turn brought it from Paganism, in which the only idea of God was of a being whose wrath must be appeased by a sacrifice. . . .
>
> Consider further what reconciliation means. It means a change on the part of the one reconciled. If one has enmity in his heart towards another, a radical change must take place in him before he is reconciled. This is the case with man. "If any man be in Christ he is a new creature: old things are passed away; behold, all things are become new. And all things are of God, who hath reconciled us to Himself by Jesus Christ." 2 Cor. v. 17, 18. But to speak of the necessity for God to be reconciled to man, is not only to say that He cherished enmity in His heart, but to say that God was partially in the wrong, and that a change had to take place in Him as well as in man. If it were not in the innocence of ignorance that men talked about

24. Waggoner, "Saved by His Life," *Present Truth*, 6 Oct. 1892, p. 308.

> God's having been reconciled to man, it would be blasphemy. That is one of the "great things and blasphemies" that the Papacy has spoken against God. Let us not echo it.[25]

Waggoner had lost sight of the objective atonement. If the reconciliation wrought by Christ means changing the heart of the sinner from its enmity against God, as Waggoner argued, how could he explain Paul's statement that the reconciliation took place historically at Calvary while men were still God's enemies (Rom. 5:10). The reconciliation of the cross was clearly a substitutionary work done on our behalf.

Good Christian theologians have never taught that God cherished enmity in His heart toward *sinners*. Waggoner was only erecting a straw man. Orthodox Christianity has taught that man's *sin* has incurred God's wrath. Sin is an offense against the majesty of God. And the law of His government guarantees that in holy wrath He will take action against sin.[26]

But Waggoner denied the propitiation of God's wrath in the sacrifice of Christ (Rom. 3:25).

> Sometimes this idea of propitiating the wrath of God has taken an easier form,—that is, easier for the worshippers. Instead of sacrificing themselves, they have sacrificed others. Human sacrifices have always been to a greater or less extent connected with heathenism. Men shudder as they read of the human sacrifices offered by the ancient inhabitants of Mexico and Peru, and by the Druids: but professed (not real) Christianity has its awful list. Even so-called Christian England has made hun-

---

25. Waggoner, "Why Did Christ Die?" p. 386.

26. See Ellen G. White, *Selected Messages*, 1:273; idem, *The Desire of Ages*, p. 753; idem, Manuscript 21, 1891, cited in *The Seventh-day Adventist Bible Commentary*, 6:1070-71; idem, Manuscript 145, 1897, cited in *Seventh-day Adventist Bible Commentary*, 6:1070.

> dreds of burnt offerings of men, for the purpose of turning away the wrath of God from the country. Wherever there is religious persecution to any degree, it springs from the mistaken idea that God demands a victim. This is shown by the words of Christ to His disciples: "The time cometh, that whosoever killeth you will think that he doeth God service." John xvi. 2. All such worship has been devil worship, and not worship of the true God.
>
> Just here somebody has remembered that it is said in Heb. ix. 22, "Without the shedding of blood there is no remission;" and this makes him think that after all God did demand a sacrifice before He would pardon man. It is very difficult for the mind to rid itself of the idea received as a legacy from Paganism, through the Papacy, that God was so angry at man for having sinned, that He could not be mollified without seeing blood flow; but that it made no difference to Him whose blood it was, if only somebody was killed: and that since Christ's life was worth more than the lives of all men, He accepted Him as a substitute for them. This is almost a brutal way of stating the case, but it is the only way that the case can be truly presented. The heathen conception of God is a brutal one, as dishonouring to God as it is discouraging to man; and this heathen idea has been allowed to colour too many texts of Scripture. It is sad to think how greatly men who really loved the Lord, have given occasion to His enemies to blaspheme.[27]

Thus Waggoner tried to make a case against historical Christianity by caricaturing its view of the atonement. In this he did what many twentieth-century liberals have

---

27. Waggoner, "Why Did Christ Die?" p. 387. Cf. the following statement: "Of course the idea of a propitiation or sacrifice is that there is wrath to be appeased. But take particular notice that it is we who require the sacrifice, and not God. He provides the sacrifice. The idea that God's wrath has to be propitiated, in order that we may have forgiveness, finds no warrant in the Bible. It is the height of absurdity to say that God is so angry with man that He will not forgive them unless something is provided to appease His wrath, and that therefore He Himself offers the gift to Himself, by which He is appeased" (Waggoner, "Justice of Mercy," p. 549).

done. But when God took action against sin at the cross, He did not punish an innocent third party. "God was in Christ, reconciling the world unto Himself" (2 Cor. 5:19). God the Lawgiver, the One wronged by human sin, bore the penalty Himself in the person of His Son.

Waggoner went on to explain his mystical atonement as follows:

> But how is it that the shedding of blood, even the blood of Christ, can take away sins? Simply because the blood is the life. "For the life of the flesh is in the blood; and I have given it to you upon the altar to make an atonement for your souls for it is the blood that maketh atonement for the soul." Lev. xvii. 11. So when we read that apart from the shedding of blood there is no remission, we know it means that no sins can be taken away except by the life of Christ. In Him is no sin: therefore when He imparts His life to a soul, that soul is at once cleansed from sin. . . .
>
> Christ came to impart the life of God to men, for it is that that they lack. The lives of all the angels in heaven could not have met the demands of the case; not because God was so inexorable, but because they could not have imparted any life to man. They had no life in themselves, but only the life that Christ imparted to them. But God was in Christ, and in Him God's everlasting life could be given to every one who would receive it. Remember that in giving His Son, God gave Himself, and you will see that a sacrifice was not demanded to satisfy God's outraged feelings, but that, on the contrary, God's inexpressible love led Him to sacrifice Himself, in order to break down man's enmity, and reconcile us to Himself.
>
> "But why could He not give us His life without dying?" That is to say, Why could He not give us His life, and still not give it? We needed life, and Christ alone had life to give; but the giving of life is dying. His death reconciles us to God, provided we make it our own by faith. We are reconciled to God by the death of Christ, because in dying He gave up His life, and He gave it to us. Being made partakers of the life of God, through faith in Christ's death, we are at peace with Him, because one life is in us both. Then we are "saved by His life." Christ

> died, but He still lives, and His life in us keeps us united to God. The imparting of His life to us frees us from sin and the continuing of it in us, keeps us from sin.[28]

Imputation, punishment and the wrath of God were all absent from Waggoner's thinking. He had largely confused the Holy Spirit's work in us with Christ's work for us.

In his article, "The Cross and Crosses," Waggoner came to the inevitable end of dehistoricizing the cross. He confounded the historic cross of Golgotha, where Christ paid for our sins, with the cross of suffering and self-denial that the believer bears as he follows Jesus. Waggoner began his article with these significant remarks: "The failure with many people is that they make a distinction between the cross of Christ and their own crosses."[29] He was apparently determined to erase all distinctions. He had already removed all distinctions between justification and sanctification, law and gospel, the work of God and the work of the believer in sanctification, and Christ's work for us and His work in us. Now Waggoner wanted to erase the distinction between what Christ did historically and vicariously on the cross and what the Holy Spirit does when He inspires us to follow Jesus in suffering, hardship and self-denial. The cross was dehistoricized and internalized. Looking at the cross for salvation meant looking to an existential experience of cross-bearing within.

Waggoner concluded his article:

> Christ is the present Saviour of all men. He is the "Lamb slain from the foundation of the world." John

---

28. Waggoner, "Why Did Christ Die?" p. 388.

29. E. J. Waggoner, "The Cross and Crosses," *Present Truth*, 22 Feb. 1894, p. 115.

> says, "If any man sin, we have an Advocate [or Comforter] with the Father, Jesus Christ the righteous; and He is the propitiation [sacrifice] for our sins." 1 John ii. 1, 2. Him "God hath set forth to be a propitiation [sacrifice] through faith in His blood." Rom. iii. 24. His blood is now shed for us: He is now lifted up for us. The knowledge that the cross is set up in every heart, that He is crucified for us, makes a delight of the crosses which come to us, all the burdens to be borne, all the habits to be given up, which are as taking our life, because they are our life. The knowledge that now Christ is crucified for us, that now are we crucified with Him, not in fancy but in fact, makes the presence of the cross a joy to us, for there we find Christ, and are brought into fellowship with His death, and live with Him. Being reconciled by His blood, we know we shall be saved by His life. To take up the cross is to take Him. To deny self is to own Him. To crucify self indeed is to take His life, and the life we live with Him is not one of hardness and discomfort and the performance of disagreeable duties for the sake of joy by and by, but it is the constant springing up of life and joy; so that with joy and not groaning we draw water from the wells of salvation.[30]

Waggoner used the biblical texts on the cross of Christ, but he meant an individual cross. This was in 1894. Later he explicitly taught that Christ is crucified and risen in every man. In order to be saved men only have to confess that Christ is already bearing their sin in them.

On the Incarnation

Waggoner's mystical atonement was inseparably connected with his view of the incarnation. We have already

---

30. Ibid., p. 117.

seen how he taught that Christ came in a sinful human nature possessing all the sinful passions and evil tendencies common to all men. Stressing the valid truth of Christ's unity with the fallen race, Waggoner failed to preserve the distinction between the humanity of Christ and the humanity of all other men. Indeed, he insisted there was no distinction.

Waggoner's pantheism came to explicit confession in 1894 in direct connection with his view on the incarnation. He said the incarnation means that Christ has come in sinful flesh. Waggoner dehistoricized the incarnation just as he had dehistoricized the atonement. As far as he was concerned, the incarnation was not a unique, once-and-for-all and unrepeatable event at Bethlehem. He placed a deliberately existential meaning on 1 John 4:2, 3:

> Hereby know ye the Spirit of God: Every spirit that confesseth that Jesus Christ is come in the flesh is of God: and every spirit that confesseth not that Jesus Christ is come in the flesh is not of God: and this is that spirit of antichrist, whereof ye have heard that it should come; and even now already is it in the world.

The antichrist, said Waggoner, is one who denies that Christ is now come in sinful flesh—all sinful flesh everywhere—and that He lives personally in every man. Waggoner had a propensity for blurring all distinctions. He even blurred the distinction between believer and unbeliever with respect to the indwelling Christ.

Waggoner's pantheistic incarnation was consistent with his effective or internal justification and his mystical or internal atonement. He first explicitly stated this position on the incarnation in an article entitled "Confessing Christ in the Flesh." It was a dissertation on 1 John 4:2, 3.

In this article Waggoner first reiterated that Christ

came in sinful flesh. He deliberately construed the statement that Christ came to dwell "among us" to mean that Christ came to dwell "in us" (John 1:14). Since God must sustain the lives of all men, he argued that the very "life of God" is in all men. Waggoner then invoked the mystical view of atonement by saying that Christ bears sin since He is in all men even when they sin.

> That life of Christ is in every man that comes into the world, the life by which he lives and moves, and it is that which every man uses and perverts in the commission of sin. So that every sin committed in the flesh since the fall of Adam is a sin charged up to the Lord Jesus Christ. It is laid on Him. . . .
>
> So we have this glorious fact, the confession of which will lift the soul up to God, the fact that Jesus Christ is come in the flesh, that all iniquity is laid upon Him and charged up to Him, and that He bears all the weaknesses and sinful tendencies of the flesh of man. He accepts it. And He still bears it, neither will He lay it off until He comes "the second time without sin unto salvation." Heb. ix. 28.
>
> This being a fact by the word of God, whosoever confesses the fact, whosoever "confesseth that Jesus Christ is come in the flesh, is of God," and whosoever "confesseth not that Jesus Christ is come in the flesh is not of God." But it is a fact whether it is confessed or not. It is a glorious truth,—one with which one can go to the outcast and tempted,—that although Christ has "gone into heaven, and is on the right hand of God; angels and authorities and powers being made subject unto Him," yet He still abides with men. Before the first advent His life was the light of men, and upon Him was laid the iniquity of all. And when He came to earth revealed as a man, it was simply in the line of giving to us a larger manifestation of the fact, and showing to us what God in the flesh, unhindered and not denied, means.[31]

---

31. Waggoner, "Confessing Christ in the Flesh," p. 151.

Waggoner did not explicitly deny the historical incarnation. He saw it only as a larger manifestation of a continual incarnation.[32] Waggoner combined this internalistic incarnation with his internalistic atonement.

> Therefore when from the heart we confess the fact which the Scripture tells us, that Jesus Christ is come in the flesh even now, and even in us, because we are in the flesh, the recognition of that brings also the other fact with it, that in Him was no sin while in the flesh; therefore His life, while we confess it, cleanses us from sin. . . .
>
> "For Christ also hath once suffered for sins, the just for the unjust, that He might bring us to God." 1 Pet. iii. 18. It was in order that we might abide in Him, and His life be perfectly manifested in us. That part of it Christ has performed. "I in them," yes, in sinful flesh. Now He wants us to acknowledge that fact continually, that we may thus be in Him. He in us means that He has taken all of our sins and carried our sorrows,—that our burdens are upon Him, and that He feels them. We in Him means that we are made "the righteousness of God in Him," and that all His righteousness which He had in the flesh is ours. All our sin is His, all His righteousness is ours. He in us to bear the sin, that we may bear the righteousness.
>
> There is everlasting glory and life in that confession; for "this is life eternal that they might know Thee, the only true God, and Jesus Christ whom Thou hast sent." John xvii. 3. This weakness of ours He feels; for Christ is come in the flesh. This sin He has borne. He knows all about it. Not only did He bear it then, but He bears it still, since it is His life that He has given us. He gave it to us, because He "tasted death for every man," and it is His life that feels and meets the pressure of this sinful flesh of ours. Those evil desires, that thirst for liquor,

---

32. "From the manger in Bethlehem shine the rays that shall fill the earth with the glory of the Lord; and that coming glory will be hastened as the manger is multiplied by the repetition of the mystery of the birth of Christ in all who receive him" (E. J. Waggoner, "The Manger and the Cross," *Review and Herald*, 6 Jan. 1903, p. 9).

> that craving of appetite, the longings of the flesh,—He has felt it all, and even now identifies Himself with us, and says, "I know that. It touches Me. I am come in the flesh, have identified Myself with it, and every sin is laid on Me." . . .
>
> "Every spirit that confesseth not that Jesus Christ is come in the flesh is not of God." It is not every spirit that says that it is not a fact; not every spirit in whom it is not a fact; for it is a fact. But every spirit that does not confess that Christ is come—not *has come*, but now *is come* —is not of God. It is always *now*. And when we confess this fact, that Jesus Christ identifies Himself with us in our sinfulness, He also confesses us before the Father in His righteousness, and we are one with Him. So the righteousness of faith speaketh on this wise, "Say not in thine heart, Who shall ascend into heaven? (that is to bring Christ down from above:)" He is come down in the likeness of sinful flesh. "Or, Who shall descend into the deep? (that is to bring up Christ again from the dead.)" He is risen. "But what saith it? The word is nigh thee, even in thy mouth and in thy heart: that is, the word of faith which we preach; that if thou shalt confess with thy mouth the Lord Jesus, and shalt believe in thine heart that God hath raised Him from the dead, thou shalt be saved." Rom. x. 6-9. Confess what?—That Jesus Christ is come in the flesh. There is something in that which every man in this world may lay hold of and find in it a lifting up.[33]

Waggoner then combined an internalistic atonement with his pantheistic sanctification. It is Christ, he said, who speaks in us to rebuke Satan and who keeps the Sabbath in us. The distinction between the work of Christ and the work of the believer was lost in the fog of Waggoner's super-spirituality.

Regarding those who fail to confess that Christ is in them and who sin, Waggoner said: "Whose life were we

---

33. Waggoner, "Confessing Christ in the Flesh," p. 150.

prostituting all the years that we have lived in sin? It was the life of Christ."[34]

In his article of July 12, 1894, Waggoner declared that "the eternal power and Divinity of God are manifest in every man." Then, speaking of creation, Waggoner blurred the distinction between the exhibition of God's power in creation and His personal life and power manifested in the gospel.

> We have seen that in every created thing the power of God is manifested. And we also learned from the scripture studied last week that the Gospel is "the power of God unto salvation." God's power is ever the same, for the text before us speaks of "His eternal power." The power, therefore, which is manifested in the things which God has made, is the same power that works in the hearts of men to save them from sin and death. Therefore we may be assured that God has constituted every portion of His universe a preacher of the Gospel. So then men may not only know the fact of God's existence, from the things which He has made, but they may know His eternal power to save them. The twentieth verse of the first chapter of Romans is an expansion of the sixteenth. It tells us how we may know the power of the Gospel. . . .
>
> With the knowledge that that which the heavens declare is the Gospel of Christ, which is the power of God unto salvation, we can easily follow the nineteenth Psalm through. It seems to the casual reader that there is a break in the continuity of this Psalm. From talking about the heavens, the writer suddenly begins to speak of the perfection of the law of God, and its converting power. "The law of the Lord is perfect, converting the soul; the testimony of the Lord is sure, making wise the simple." Verse 7. But there is no break at all. The law of God is the righteousness of God, and the Gospel reveals the righteousness of God, and the heavens declare the Gospel; therefore it follows that the heavens reveal the righteous-

34. Ibid., p. 152.

ness of God. "The heavens declare His righteousness, and all the people see His glory." Ps. xcvii. 6. The glory of God is His goodness, because we are told that it is through sin that men come short of His glory. Rom. iii. 23. Therefore we may know that whoever looks upon the heavens with reverence, seeing in them the power of the Creator, and will yield himself to that power, will receive the saving righteousness of God. Even the sun, moon, and stars, whose light is but a part of the glory of the Lord, will shine righteousness into his soul.[35]

---

35. E. J. Waggoner, "Studies in Romans: God's Revelation to Man," *Present Truth*, 12 July 1894, p. 438. Cf. "Truth is implanted in the heavens and earth; it fills the stars, and keeps them in their places; it is that by which the plants grow, and the birds build their nests; it is that by which they know how to find their way across the sea" (E. J. Waggoner, "The Blotting Out of Sin," *Review and Herald*, 30 Sept. 1902, p. 8).

9

Waggoner the Pantheist

The General Conference of 1897

E. J. Waggoner first expressed his pantheistic ideas in 1894. In 1895 and 1896 he did not significantly develop these ideas but repeated his thoughts on justification, the atonement and the incarnation. Then in 1897 Waggoner returned to the United States from England for the General Conference session.[1] Here he presented a series of studies on the book of Hebrews. He ignored those chapters so vital to Adventist theology—apparently because he no longer believed in a literal sanctuary in heaven nor in its "cleansing" through the intercession of Christ.[2] Rather than provoking a confrontation on something so vital to historic Adventism, however, Waggoner focused on the earlier chapters of Hebrews. We are tempted to say he used this scripture to promote his pantheistic sentiments.

Amazingly, none of the General Conference delegates

1. Held in College View, Lincoln, Nebraska.
2. E. J. Waggoner, *A "Confession of Faith,"* pp. 14-15.

or leaders of the church protested Waggoner's pantheism. In fact, his remarks were apparently well received. Furthermore, Robert Haddock is the only scholar we know who has detected Waggoner's pantheism at the 1897 General Conference session. Froom notes that Waggoner spoke at the session but makes no mention of his pantheism. He accuses Kellogg, however, of then introducing the theories which later had their effect on Waggoner.

In his lecture on February 11, 1897, Waggoner said:

> All things stand by his Word. He spoke, and it was. So when we look abroad on the things of nature, we see evidences of his power. When we look over the meadow, we see the Word of God made grass. God spake, and, lo! that Word appeared as a tree, or as grass. . . .
>
> As the last act of creation, God made man. And as in all creation we see the Word of God made trees, grass, etc., in man we see the Word of God made flesh. . . .
>
> So just as God made man, and crowned him with glory and honor, we now see the man Jesus, that Man who is in every man crowned with honor and glory; and he added all things unto him.[3]

In his following address Waggoner continued:

> When God made Adam by his Word, the Word was made flesh. As God spoke all things into existence, his words went forth, and, lo! the earth appeared. His Word went forth; he spoke; he said, Trees, and they were there; he said, Grass, and it was; so that all these things that grow over the ground are visible manifestations of the Word. It is the Word of life, and these are simply some of the various forms of the life of the Word. And so with man formed there in the beginning. There we see the Word manifested as flesh. The power by which this was

---

3. E. J. Waggoner, "Studies in the Book of Hebrews," no. 3, *General Conference Daily Bulletin* 1, no. 3 (16 Feb. 1897): 34-5.

done was God's power, and so God was in the Word, and the Word was in Adam, so that this power could be manifested in him, God dwelling in him and working in him; God taking this dust and using it to do these wonderful things. It is God that worketh in you to will and to do his good pleasure. Now, if God is there, and I am here, that is altogether too far away. It is God that worketh in me. The Word was made flesh, and the life of Adam was the life of God. He has no other life. Now the blessedness of this is, when man fell, the Word was made flesh. But suppose God had forsaken him, and had not been willing to make the Word flesh; what would have become of him?—He would have returned to dust. But God continues his life to man. So when man fell, God goes right down there with him. Is that so, or is it some fancy? Did God continue life to man, notwithstanding he had sinned? We are here, are we not? We are sinners. We are living, are we not? Whose life is it manifested in us?—It is God's life. Then God continues his life to sinful men. When sin entered, death came; so when man sinned, death came upon him. God stayed with him; therefore, in that he stayed with man, although man had sinned, God took upon himself sinful flesh. And so he took upon himself death, for death had passed upon all the world.

Now, let us see further. All creation is continued until now "by the same Word." Everything in this world is kept by the same Word. Although everything is cursed, and everybody can see that, it is yet a fact that it continues; it is an evidence that God is there, Christ is there, the divine Word is there bearing the curse. But in what thing does Christ endure the curse? Where is that point where the curse falls upon Christ?—Sinful flesh. Not only sinful flesh, but that which stands as the symbol of the curse that falls upon Christ—the cross. What is the evidence that he bears the curse?—"Accursed is every one that hangeth on a tree." Death and the cross both together mean the curse; therefore wherever there is anything, there is the curse. Nevertheless, wherever there is anything, there is Christ. Wherever there is anything, then, that exists and bears the curse, there is Christ. But where Christ has the curse upon him, he bears the cross. Then do you not see the truthfulness of that statement which appeared from Sister White about a year ago, that "the cross of Christ is stamped upon every leaf in the forest?" And a little later than a year ago there appeared in a first-page article of the *Review and Herald* a statement that the very bread we eat is stamped with the cross. There is something wonderful in that. Perhaps when you read that in every blade, and every leaf, there is the cross of Christ, some of us read it over without thinking about it, and some of us simply said, with Nicodemus, how can this be? How soon do we find Christ crucified, then?—Just as soon as there was any curse. And he is risen again as well, because if you preach Christ crucified, his resurrection necessarily goes with that.

Now, see how God has proclaimed the gospel for our encouragement everywhere. People are inclined to get discouraged; Christians are likely to think, Well, the Lord has forgotten us. Did you ever think that way, as though the Lord didn't care for you;—that he has left you alone? Is there any one who has not felt that way, discouraged, in short? I am not of much importance in this world, we sometimes say; I am of no consequence; I am only one very insignificant and despised, and justly despised; I could drop out, and it wouldn't make any difference. He said that not a sparrow can fall to the ground without his notice; and why?—Because the life of God is there, and there is nothing that can come upon anything in this world that God does not feel. It touches him personally, because his life is all the sensibility that there is in this world. You are struck, you are beaten; you feel it. What makes you feel it? If you were dead you wouldn't feel it. Why do you feel it?—Because you are alive. Where do you get life?—It comes from God. It is God's own life isn't it? Then is it possible for a human being to be touched, just touched—not beaten, bruised, or despised—and the Lord not feel it? Can it be so, whether saint or sinner? Can anything happen to any creature in this world does God not feel? Whither shall I go from his presence, and where shall I go to be away from the presence of God? We cannot get away, because God's power is in everything; and therefore a sparrow cannot fall to the ground without the Lord knowing it. We live with all these infirmities. That is Christ in the flesh, then. Do you suppose that Christ

> would have endured all this, and stayed here all these years, with all this infirmity and wickedness and weakness and sin upon him, and then by and by step out and let it all drop? If he was to do that, he would have let it drop in the beginning; but the fact that he came in fallen humanity is an evidence of God's presence, and his presence to give life. And so God on everything has put the stamp of the cross,—upon every leaf, upon every blade of grass, upon everything that we have to do with. He simply means that everywhere we go, and everything we have to do, and everything we eat, and the air we breathe,—through these he is simply preaching the gospel to us, giving the gospel to us. Encouragement, strength, salvation![4]

Waggoner's presentation on February 15 revealed the link between his pantheism and his view of the incarnation. He said:

> Christ has come in the flesh, my flesh. Why? Is it because I am so good?—O, no; for there is no good flesh for Christ to come into. Christ has come in the flesh, in every man's flesh. "That was the true Light, which lighteth every man that cometh into the world." The life is the light, and lights every man. In other words, every man in this world lives upon the grace of God. "It is of the Lord's mercies that we are not consumed;" and that is true of the man who blasphemes God. Where did that man get his breath?—From God. God continues breath to him in his wickedness, in order that the gift may reveal God's goodness and he repent: for it is the goodness of God. He is kind to the evil and the good; he sends rain upon the just and the unjust; that is God.[5]

Waggoner then removed the distinction between the

---

4. E. J. Waggoner, "Studies in the Book of Hebrews," no. 4, *General Conference Daily Bulletin* 1, no. 3 (16 Feb. 1897): 45-6.

5. E. J. Waggoner, "Studies in the Book of Hebrews," no. 6, *General Conference Daily Bulletin* 1, no. 5 (18 Feb. 1897): 70-71.

Holy Spirit and the breath from God given to all mankind in creation.

Now, there is one thing we need all the time to keep our lives going. It is air. Did you make this air? Where did you get the air you breathe? It is God's air; it is the breath of God.

God put his own breath into man's nostrils, in order that he might live. That is the way we continue to breathe. It is the breath of God that keeps us alive, the Spirit of God in our nostrils. Well, that man must acknowledge what is so patent that he cannot help but acknowledge it; namely, that he did not bring himself into existence, and that he cannot perpetuate his existence for one instant. He is brought face to face with the power of God in him, keeping him alive. It is Christ in fallen man, it is Christ in cursed man, it is Christ with the curse on him, it is Christ crucified. Christ taking fallen, sinful humanity upon him, is Christ crucified. Do not say in your heart, Who will ascend up into heaven to bring Christ down to me, that is to be crucified? No; he is here in the flesh.

"If thou wilt confess with thy mouth the Lord Jesus." What is it to confess him? To confess a thing is not to make it so, but it is to acknowledge that the thing is so. Now the fact that we are to confess is, that Christ is come in the flesh. O, let me read a word here. Rom. 1:18-20: "For the wrath of God is revealed from heaven against all ungodliness and unrighteousness of men, who hold down the truth in unrighteousness." What is the truth? Christ says, "I am the truth." Thus the truth that is stated is that "the wrath of God is revealed from heaven against all ungodliness and unrighteousness of men" who hold back Christ in them. "Because that which may be known of God is manifest in them; for God hath shewed it unto them;" for ever since the creation of the world, the invisible things of God are clearly seen, "being understood by the things that are made."

Look at the trees; we see the power and the divinity of God in the trees and grass, and in every thing that God has made, and see it clearly, too. But I read that text for years, and forgot that I was one of the things that God made. Am I not one of the things of the creation, just as well as a tree? Then what is seen and understood in the things that God has made, even man not excluded?—His eternal power and divinity. So we are without excuse. Now if thou wilt confess with thy mouth the Lord Jesus, that he is in your flesh,—but do not stop with that confession,—"and shalt believe in thy heart that God has raised him from the dead," lifted him up to his own right hand in the heavenly places, "thou shalt be saved." That is Christ crucified, and raised in every man. When he will confess the truth, and believe the truth, then he has Christ in him, crucified and risen, with the resurrection power, to do whatsoever God says.[6]

The next day Waggoner continued:

Yes, believe on the Lord. But, what? Where is he? Where may I find the Lord? How can I know about Christ crucified and risen? It does not say that. The Word is Christ. Now do not say, Who came to bring the Word to us, or Christ to us, in order that we might be made righteous to keep the law. No; what saith it?—The Word is in them. It is in thy mouth. Or, in thy mouth, and in thy heart, literally.

What is the word of faith which we preach?—"That if thou shalt confess with thy mouth the Lord Jesus, and shalt believe in thine heart that God hath raised him from the dead, thou shalt be saved." Now, what is the great fact, the great truth, about the Lord Jesus that is to be confessed with the mouth? Why, that the Word was made flesh—that is the thing to be confessed, Confess the Lord Jesus. Why confess Christ?—Because to confess a thing is to say it is so. To confess the Lord Jesus in the flesh, is to confess that Christ is the power of God; and that is to confess that this is not of men at all. This life I have is not my life. It is God's.

It is God's in the most absolute sense. The breath of God, and the Word—these are even in thy mouth. It is the

6. Ibid., pp. 71-2.

manifestation of God's power. Then when a man confesses that, he simply gives up, he renounces all his assumptions to power, and of right to rule; all ownership of himself that he has claimed to have, he gives up, and he is the Lord's because this life is the life that God has given. It is the breath that God has lent. I am living upon his bounty; not only so, but it is his life within.

Knowing that fact—that Christ, the Lord, the power of God, is in my flesh—now I will believe in my heart that God has raised him from the dead; that is, gives him the victory over the infirmity of the flesh, even over death. Then I have Christ crucified and risen again in the flesh, and when I believe in that Christ risen to the right hand of God, that lifts me up so long as I believe. With the heart man believeth unto righteousness. . . .

We often speak of the third angel's message going with power, or with a loud voice, "the loud cry." What have we here?—"Lift up thy voice with strength; lift it up, be not afraid." Then this is the loud cry of the third angel's message. This is what we have here in the fortieth chapter of Isaiah. It is the last message going with a loud cry, saying, "Say unto the cities of Judah, Behold your God." Where? says one. I cannot see him; where is he? Get your eyes open then. That is the last message, Behold your God. Where?—In the things which he has made.

We may learn lessons from the grass. How often we have gone out just as the grass or the Indian corn was beginning to spring forth, and as we passed along we noticed a big clod of earth detached and rising up. It might weigh several pounds. And then we had the curiosity to look under it; and what did we see?—just a little blade of grass, perhaps a blade of wheat, so tiny and small it had no color to it yet;—just a little white mass of fiber and water; that is all, nothing to it. It was just standing upright, and not only standing upright under that clod of earth, but it was steadily pushing it out of the way, and was just keeping its place and going right along, regardless of this clod. It is safe to say that a blade of grass pushes away a weight ten thousand times its own weight. If a man had as much power according to his size and weight, he could lift a mountain; he could take up Pike's Peak, and throw it off as a lad would a football.

But when you take it out of there, it will not hold itself up. It just yields—it is gone. If you even remove the clod, it cannot stand. That blade of grass is not such a little thing after all, but it is undeniable that there was a wonderful power manifested in that blade of grass. But what was that power?—God's own life, his own personal presence there, doing in the grass just what he designed for the grass; it was God that was working in it, both to will and to do of his own good pleasure. . . .

What life therefore is manifested everywhere in the universe?—The life of Christ. Christ in the flesh crucified and risen, Christ in the flesh crucified in me, because if Christ is crucified some distance from me, even though it be close beside me, it is far away. I cannot make the connection. But when I know that that life which was offered, and which was powerful enough to gain the victory over sin and death, that very same life is in me, and confess it and believe it, everything that that life can do is mine. . . .

So we see that the law is one, and that it is God's life, and it is not an arbitrary arrangement, but God is the author and source of life, and his life works in all his creatures so far as they let him.[7]

On February 17 Waggoner completely dehistoricized the atonement and replaced it with the sin bearing of Christ in every man.

Now what we want is to stop trifling. If the Lord is so near, and to be found, we want to find him; and he says: Seek ye the Lord while he is near. While he may be found, call upon him. While he is near, O, so near that you do not have to go across the room; you do not have to go anywhere at all but here; he is within you. He was so near me all those years that I did not know anything about him, and he was bearing my sin. Why?—Because the Lord Jesus is in everything that he has made. He upholds all

7. E. J. Waggoner, "Studies in the Book of Hebrews," no. 7, *General Conference Daily Bulletin* 1, no. 6 (19 Feb. 1897): 85-9.

things, because he is in them. He is cohesion even to inanimate nature. It is the personal, powerful presence of God that keeps the mountains together, and the stones from crumbling to pieces; because God is there with his personal power. And we saw yesterday about the grass, and the trees, and the rootlets,—that they take up the nourishment that is adapted to them, and leave to one side that which is not fitted for them. That fine discrimination which takes what is necessary for them, and leaves the other aside, we saw was nothing but the power of God doing for them just what we say is instinct in the animals; and when it comes to man, we call it reason. That is God's personal presence. Now if we acknowledge that he is in us, that we are as grass and plants, and acknowledge that as truly as the grass itself does, then this power of God will lead us to make just the same right choice as does the grass, the rootlet, and the tree, in choosing that which is necessary for them. . . .

When we believe that all flesh is grass, we simply allow God in us to choose for us as he chooses in the rootlet and the plant, to select that thing which is necessary. The rootlet will go a long distance in search of what it needs, and will find it every time. It will go a long distance to find moisture, and leave the dry place alone. It is passive in the hands of the Lord, and the Lord chooses for it, and it is simply right.

We are to learn this truth, to behold God in the things he has made. Thus we are to behold God in us. . . .

Crucified and risen in the flesh, in every man's flesh, I carry to the people that message, Behold your God, crucified and risen, not far from you, but in your mouth and heart; believe that he is your life, that he was crucified and has risen to deliver you from death and sin. When we recognize that, then he will fill us.[8]

On February 18 Waggoner continued:

What is air, then?—It is God's breath. If we knew this

---

8. E. J. Waggoner, "Studies in the Book of Hebrews," no. 8, *General Conference Daily Bulletin* 1, no. 7 (22 Feb. 1897): 101-2, 104.

not only physically, but spiritually, we should be much more alive than we are. . . .

The life that God breathed into man was God, and so long as man continued to acknowledge that his life, his breath, came from God, he remained good.[9]

Waggoner logically combined his pantheism with his view of sanctification.

What is righteousness?—Doing right. Then many shall do right; that is clear. And how will many do right?—By the obedience of One. Well, then, if I am made righteous by his obedience, if I do right by his obedience, where does he obey?—In me. What am I doing?—Letting him, submitting to the righteousness of God. . . .

Then, when Christ in us obeys,—mark, when Christ *in us* obeys,—how much power has the devil against us?—None. When we allow Christ to fill us through the Spirit, so that we are filled with all the fullness of God, then we have power "over all the power of the enemy." What is our part?—Submission.

Now, that same work of submission is enough for you and me all the rest of our lives. To submit, to give up, and to keep giving up, or rather, to keep *given up*, as new experiences arise, is all we have to do; and it will occupy all our time. There is work enough for us, then, to hold still, and let the Lord fill us with his Spirit, and work us. That does not mean laziness; it is passive activity, if you please; it means being just as active as the Lord himself was; because Christ himself living in us will be just the same as he was when he was here on the earth. . . .

Then God will live in us, and will choose for us just the same as in the tree. We do not know anything, but he will think for us. . . .

. . . but he will think in us everything that he desires us to think, and will work in us perfectly to will and to do his good pleasure. Then we will be organized, reorganized,

9. E. J. Waggoner, "Studies in the Book of Hebrews," no. 9, *General Conference Daily Bulletin* 1, no. 10 (25 Feb. 1897): 158.

made new. It is God thinking and acting in us.[10]

Here pantheism, quietism and perfectionism were all blended. The distinction between the Creator and His work, on the one hand, and the creature and his work, on the other, was lost. Waggoner's theology blurred all important distinctions. Like the great Eastern religions, it finally removed the distinction between the Creator and the creature. Many people rather innocently express an extreme view of sanctification which sounds very pious and spiritual but which in reality is pantheistic. How familiar is this pantheistic statement from Waggoner on February 21, 1897!

> His victory is our victory, because he gained it for us, and we get the benefit of it by allowing him to dwell in us in his fullness. The enemy is just as powerless against Christ in us, as he was against Christ eighteen hundred years ago.[11]

On March 2 Waggoner declared: "God himself is personally present in all his works. He himself is the energy that is manifest in all creation. God himself is force, the force that is manifest in all matter."[12]

Waggoner expressed his pantheistic perfectionism in a sermon to the conference on Sabbath morning, March 6.

> If anything less than the fulness of God be in us, we cannot witness for him. God's faithful witnesses, seen in the starry heavens, bear continual testimony to his glory; but they speak no word. So with us. The strongest witness we can bear to the character of God, is a life that is

---

10. Ibid., pp. 156-57, 159.

11. E. J. Waggoner, "Studies in the Book of Hebrews," no. 10, *General Conference Daily Bulletin* 1, no. 13 (2 Mar. 1897): 210.

12. E. J. Waggoner, "Studies in Hebrews," no. 18, *General Conference Bulletin* 2, no. 1 (First Quarter, 1897): 13.

consistent with that character. And this is not true of the preachers only, but of every child of God. And this life can only be lived through the power of the Spirit of Christ dwelling in us. . . .

The power of God is in the truth. We do not seek for miracles, but we should seek for the transforming power of the Spirit of God. The power of God in us seeks for utterance and expression. It has been too long repressed. The Lord still waits for us. He does not become impatient with us; and bears with us because he has his character at stake. The only way in which he can demonstrate the perfection of his character, and take away his reproach, is in perfecting a people to his praise. He is able to accomplish this in us. Shall we let God have a chance? Shall we let the people know that God is with us, that they may see him and know him?[13]

The General Conference of 1899

E. J. Waggoner was a key speaker at the General Conference again in 1899.[14] Here he carried his pantheism into the area of health reform.

On February 19 Waggoner affirmed that the energy and cohesion in the natural world is "the life of the Lord Jesus Christ,—the Spirit of God."[15]

On the morning of February 21 Waggoner confessed that in the last few months the Lord had taught him "how to live forever."[16] Then he announced, "I expect to live forever."[17] He was not talking about possessing eter-

13. E. J. Waggoner, "Witnesses for God," *General Conference Bulletin* 2, no. 1 (First Quarter, 1897): 55, 57.

14. Held in South Lancaster, Massachusetts.

15. E. J. Waggoner, in *Daily Bulletin of the General Conference* 8, no. 5 (21 Feb. 1899): 42.

16. E. J. Waggoner, in *Daily Bulletin of the General Conference* 8, no. 6 (22 Feb. 1899): 53.

17. Ibid.

nal life by faith but about possessing it in reality. Waggoner had lost the distinction between faith and reality. If Christ lived in our sinful flesh just as He had lived in Palestine, the life of Christ in us would live as sinlessly and as free from disease as when He lived in Palestine. Thus Waggoner's reasoning was consistent with his extreme view of sanctification and perfectionism. He said:

> Just as you can not conceive of Jesus' losing a day's work from sickness, so it ought not to be conceivable of Seventh-day Adventists' losing a day's work from sickness. . . . Then if the life of Jesus is manifest in our mortal flesh, we shall be in this world the same as he was.[18]

Again, Waggoner removed any real distinction between the unique Christ and the believer. In his theology the incarnation goes on happening all the time.

In the afternoon of February 21 Waggoner began to argue that simple health agencies like air, water and food have healing power because they contain the life—or blood—of Jesus Christ by which sin is cleansed and disease overcome. Waggoner said the breath of life which God gives to every man is the Holy Spirit. If a man will only believe that God's life is in the air, he will surely be filled with the Spirit.

> There was One about whom the devil could not taunt God, and that was Jesus Christ. When we ourselves see, and get other people to see, that this is God's life,—that it is his Spirit which fills all space; that air is a means of conveying his Spirit to us; and that it is God's own life,—then we see that air is the power of God to purify, to give

18. Ibid. Cf. "Suppose a man recognized that fact, and therefore let God have his own way in controlling the human body, so that he might fill it with his life. What disease could affect him? Would he not ward off all disease, as he did in Christ himself?—Certainly (E. J. Waggoner, in *Daily Bulletin of the General Conference* 8, no. 7 [23 Feb. 1899]: 58).

> life. You take in the life, and live by it; thus we see the power of the blood of Jesus Christ, which cleanses from all sin. He gives us life, to keep us going. So then, if we shut out the air, we shut out, unconsciously, the fulness of the Spirit of God. But if we receive it,—let the air come in full and free, and take it as the gift of God,—we get life. It is God that gives us this life, and we live by him. It is the same with eating. We live by the food that he gives to us; but it is his own life that he gives to us, and there is no other. If we take that by faith,—and "the just shall live by faith,"—we are receiving the life of God.[19]

Waggoner removed the distinction between figurative speech and literal speech. When the Bible uses air to represent the Spirit, Waggoner understood the passages literally. He removed the distinction between atmospheric air and the Holy Spirit.

Waggoner argued that the life of Christ is literally in food. When Christ said, "The seed is the Word," Waggoner removed the distinction between a figure of speech and literal speech. When corn is sown, he said, the Word of God is sown. Christ's life—His Word, His blood—is in the corn. So when Christ said of the sacramental bread, "This is My body," Waggoner claimed it was literally true.

Here Waggoner introduced a view on the words of institution of the Supper which he later repeated in his book, *The Everlasting Covenant.* He said the papacy pretended to change the bread into the body of Christ. Waggoner argued that the bread was already the body of Christ. In fact, all food contains the body of Christ. Waggoner acknowledged, however, that it is better to eat good food because it contains the body of Christ in a purer form.

---

19. Waggoner, *Daily Bulletin* 8, no. 7, p. 58.

A voice: Is the life of God in the bread?

E. J. Waggoner: Yes.

A voice: What is the difference, then, between this and the position taken by the priest?

E. J. Waggoner: They are diametrically opposite. Christ said, when he took bread, and broke it, "This is my body;" but the priest says, "I will take this bread, and make it the body." The priest denies the truth of God. The Lord's Supper is simply the model meal. Christ is the bread of life,—the bread that came down from heaven. But when I said that, I was not speaking of manna. The Jews said: "Our fathers had manna." What did God say before he gave the Israelites manna?—He said, "I will rain bread from heaven for them." "I am the bread that came down from heaven." Yet in that day they said to Jesus, We would like to see a miracle. What had he done?—He had brought the bread from heaven for them. He had given them bread,—himself,—and they had all been feeding upon spiritual meat.

Christ took the piece of bread, and said, "This is my body." Whoever really recognizes Christ in the bread, ought to cut off everything from his table that which is not purely of Christ, and that does not have the pure life of Christ in it. He should cut off everything from it that is corrupted, because Christ is a Lamb without blemish or spot.

Then we are to take that by faith unto life. Are we to live by faith?—"This is my body." But let every man stop, and examine himself. "He that eateth and drinketh unworthily, eateth and drinketh damnation to himself, not discerning the Lord's body." What was the trouble with the Jews in the desert?—They had spiritual meat; but the very best food in the world will not save a man if he does not see the Lord in it. The infidel can not preach the gospel of health, because when one takes these things apart from Christ, he is not made the underlying principle.

What do we put into the ground when we want corn?—We plant the seed. But what did God put there to bring forth the first corn? "The seed is the word of God." He sowed the seed of his own word. Now when you have a handful of good seed, that seed has the life of God in it.

You have got the same thing that God put into the ground when corn first grew. When this is made into bread, life is in it still. We do not see the life, but it is there, and it is the life of God. It is his body, and we take his body and get life. But if we take it, not discerning his body, we reject that, and really say we can live without him. We do not pay attention to his laws, and so die. But if you see in it his body, then in every meal to which we sit down, we see the body of Christ; and we take it, and we live by it. In every meal we eat without recognizing the Lord's body, we eat and drink condemnation to ourselves.[20]

In a discourse on February 21, Waggoner applied the same reasoning to water. Just as the Holy Spirit is imparted through the air and the body—or life—of Christ is imparted through the food, so God's life—or blood—is conveyed to us in the water. "Sparkling water . . . is God's own life flowing from his throne."[21] Waggoner continued:

Thank the Lord that the river of God is full of water, and never runs dry. It is always running. Do you not see? The rain comes down from heaven, filters down from the river of God. You and I have drunk from the rock, and have forgotten God the Rock. We have been drinking from the life of God all our lives, and have not known it. . . .

We have a drink of water here,—living water. Where does it come from?—The throne of God, where Jesus Christ, the Lamb slain, is. It flows from his heart. It is the blood of Christ, which cleanses from all sin. The blood of Christ is a real thing.

That water which flows from the throne of God is his life, and his life is the light. "If we walk in the light as he is in the light, we have fellowship with one another; and

---

20. Ibid.

21. E. J. Waggoner, "The Water of Life," *Daily Bulletin of the General Conference* 8, no. 8 (24 Feb. 1899): 79.

> the blood of the Son of God cleanses us from all sin." Is that a real thing? or is it only a figurative expression,—a mere form of words? Can we actually bathe in the blood of Christ, and live by it?—Yes; for what is the blood?—It is the life. The life is in the blood. By whatever means Christ conveys the life to us, that is the blood, the life. He gives it to us. It does not necessarily have to be always in one form. There are innumerable forms in which life is conveyed to us; but it is all the one life. Remember, the Spirit and the water and the blood agree in one; they all come to one.
>
> Water is life, and it has life-giving powers.[22]

Waggoner attained the height of fantastic pantheistic drivel when he exclaimed:

> O, I delight in drinking water, as I never have before; I delight in bathing. Why, I come right to the throne of God. A man may get righteousness in bathing, when he knows where the water comes from, and recognizes the source. The world is a good deal nearer the gospel than it knows anything about when it says that "cleanliness is next to godliness." Ah, but cleanliness is godliness. "Now ye are clean through the word which I have spoken unto you." Christ loved the church, and gave himself for it, that he might purify it and cleanse it by a "water-bath in the word." That is the way it reads in the Danish, and that is literal, too. Just bathe in the word. That is not figurative, that is not sentimental; God wants his people to live now as seeing the Invisible, so that they will walk in the sight of the river of God, and drink from the throne of God, and all they do will be eating and drinking in his presence. . . .
>
> Let us drink in the water every day. Then we are living in the presence of God.[23]

In 1889 Waggoner first lost the vital distinction be-

---

22. Ibid., p. 80.

23. Ibid.

tween the righteousness of faith and sanctification. Being logical to his premise, he proceeded to remove every vital distinction in every area of his theology. By 1899 he had lost the distinction between figure and fact. He could see no difference between literal water and spiritual water. He had become thoroughly mystical. For him all the great objective truths of Christianity, such as the incarnation and atonement, were dehistoricized and internalized.

Waggoner's heresy at the General Conference of 1899 was so outrageous that someone should have exposed it. But there is little evidence that any of the leading brethren were alarmed. In fact, W. W. Prescott was moving in Waggoner's current.[24] Although A. F. Ballenger seemed troubled by the direction he felt Waggoner was taking,[25] the only significant indication of concern was a letter Ellen G. White sent from Australia to be read at the session. She warned the delegates of subtle theories about God and nature.[26]

The General Conference of 1901

Waggoner was a speaker at the General Conference again in 1901. Mrs. White had returned from Australia and was present. W. A. Spicer had also returned from India and was alarmed to find Kellogg and others talking like Hindus. Spicer described the crisis as follows:

> Where is heaven? I was asked. I had my idea of the

---

24. W. W. Prescott, in *Daily Bulletin of the General Conference* 8, no. 7 (23 Feb. 1899): 58-60.

25. Albion F. Ballenger, in *Daily Bulletin of the General Conference* 8, no. 7 (23 Feb. 1899): 58.

26. Ellen G. White, "Special Testimony," *Daily Bulletin of the General Conference* 8, no. 16 (6 Mar. 1899): 157-60.

> center of the universe, with heaven and the throne of God in the midst, but disclaimed any attempt to fix the center of the universe astronomically. But I was urged to understand that heaven is where God is, and God is everywhere in the grass, in the trees, in all creation. There was no place in this scheme of things for angels going between heaven and earth, for heaven was here and everywhere. The cleansing of the sanctuary that we taught about was not something in a far-away heaven. The sin is here (the hand pointing to the heart), and here is the sanctuary to be cleansed. To think of God as having a form in the image of which man was made, was said to be idolatry. . . .
>
> It seemed to me these ideas set all earth and heaven and God swirling away into mist. There was in it no objective unity to lay hold of. With scripture terms and Christian ideas interwoven, it seemed the old doctrine of the Hindus—all nature a very part of Brahma, and Brahma the whole.[27]

Waggoner continued his pantheistic theme in his presentations at the General Conference. In his address on April 11 he restated his view that the life of Christ is immanent in all creation.[28] He said the life of God is in all the air, water, food and light that blesses this world. Here in 1901 he himself stated that he made no distinction between figurative and literal speech.

> Let us see some of the ways in which this life is manifested, so that we can lay hold upon it. Right here in this chapter, we have it, "God is light." I believe that. I do not have any explanation to make; I do not trouble my brain in thinking about "spiritual" or "literal" or figurative language, or anything of that kind. The Bible

---

27. W. A. Spicer, "How the Spirit of Prophecy Met a Crisis," p. 20; cited in Robert Haddock, "A History of the Doctrine of the Sanctuary in the Advent Movement: 1800-1905," pp. 335-36.

28. E. J. Waggoner, "Bible Study," *General Conference Bulletin* 4, no. 10 (14 Apr. 1901): 220-24.

says, "God is light," and I believe it. Believing that to be so, has revealed to me many things that I never would have known if I had not believed it. Is it the glory of God that he has placed upon the heavens? The heavens declare it. The sun, the moon, and the stars give light to this earth; but whose light are they giving?—The light of God. Christ is the light of the world, and when, on one occasion, he made that statement, he immediately demonstrated it so that we can see how real his light is, because he found a man born blind, and made him see. Then when your eyes look out on such a day as to-day, and see the light covering the whole earth as with a garment, what are you looking at?—Life. Whose life?—Why, the only life there is—God's life; we are seeing his life. We are too much afraid of coming into touch with realities. Let it be fixed in our minds everlastingly, that when we look out and see this glorious light, we are seeing God's face,—really seeing the light that shines from God's face.

Light is one manifestation of God's life, but in the first chapter of John we have reference to a cleansing fluid as well. We have something that cleanses us from all sin, and that is the life of the Lord, for we are "saved by his life." Turn to the thirty-sixth psalm: "How excellent is thy loving kindness, O God! therefore the children of men put their trust under the shadow of thy wings. They shall be abundantly satisfied with the fatness of thy house; and thou shalt make them drink of the river of thy pleasure. For with thee is the fountain of life; in thy light shall we see light."

So here we have water, the fountain of life. But life is light, and the river of life, clear as crystal, that flows sparkling from the throne of God, is but another manifestation of that life which is light. And so we have water as a manifestation of that one life. Water cleanses impurity; and by the daily washing of our hands, by the washing of our clothes, by the water that washes the impurities from the earth and carries them away to the sea, by that running water which will take impurities that are cast into the stream and swallowing them up, so that in the course of a few miles' running, the water will be pure again, the Lord is showing us the cleansing power of his life, so that we may know that if we simply let ourselves be lost in

> that life, we shall be cleansed and kept free from sin. This is a reality.[29]

Waggoner then repeated his fantastic views on the institution of the Supper—"This is My body"—and on the air conveying the personal life of God. Waxing spiritually romantic, he said:

> Some time ago, when I was out taking my morning walk, and the soft refreshing breeze was fanning my cheek, I remembered that the breeze that blew was the breath of God's nostrils. He was blowing his own breath upon my face. You have often thought of the wind kissing the cheek, and then that scripture came to my mind, "Let him kiss me with the kisses of his mouth, for thy love is better than wine." What a grand thing to know that one is in such close connection with it. [Voice: Amen!] This is happiness. To awaken in the morning, and to feel that life through the whole body, and to know that I am in personal connection with it, to know that God is not only in that room, round about me, but that his life is in me.[30]

In this address Waggoner acknowledged that some regarded his views as pantheistic. But he denied the charge.[31] It is true that his views were not the cruder kind of heathen pantheism which identifies the created thing with the Creator. They were a more refined pantheism that saw God as immanent in all creation so that the work of God was confused with the work of the creature.

By 1901 Waggoner had so internalized the Christian religion that he had lost sight of the transcendent God.

29. Ibid., p. 221.
30. Ibid., p. 222.
31. Ibid., p. 223.

The throne of God was man.[32] Waggoner's concept of the human nature of Christ was prominently bound to his pantheistic sentiments.[33] He obviously did not understand the error in Rome's doctrine of the "immaculate conception." He thought Rome mistakenly attributed a sinless human nature to Christ.[34] In reality, however, this is the faith of historic Christianity. Rome erroneously ascribes Christ's sinless nature to the supposed sinlessness of Mary rather than to the power of the Holy Spirit which sanctified Christ's human nature in the womb of the virgin.

One more point in Waggoner's thought of 1901 must be noted because it represents a prominent school of thought we will again encounter in this decade of the 1970's. That is Waggoner's perfectionism applied to the final generation.

Waggoner again expressed his extreme view of sanctification, which he linked to his view on "Christ in sinful flesh." Christ has demonstrated, he said, that God can live a sinless life in sinful flesh. We cannot live a sinless life, but God can do it in us just as He did it in the historic Jesus. This is what God will do in the final generation. Then Waggoner added:

> What is man made for?—For the dwelling-place of God. . . .
>
> When man, who is the throne of God, has the Spirit of God fully dwelling in him, that one universal, undivided Spirit thinks God's thoughts in him, just the same as when my brain thinks, my foot moves. . . .
>
> The perfect man is the man who does not think for him-

---

32. E. J. Waggoner, "Sermon," *General Conference Bulletin* 4, no. 6 (9 Apr. 1901): 145-50.

33. E. J. Waggoner, "Sermon," *General Conference Bulletin* 4, no. 17 (22 Apr. 1901): 403-8.

34. Ibid., p. 404.

> self, but lets God do his thinking for him.[35]

This extreme view of sanctification is essentially pantheistic. It blurs the distinction between what God does and what the creature does. Man is a person. Union with God does not mean God does everything in man. A man's acts of believing, obeying, praying and working are really *his own acts*, and we must not lose sight of this. Although it may be given man of God to do these things, they are man's own acts. Even the expulsion of sin is the act of the soul itself.[36]

To say believers today live exactly the same life that Jesus lived removes the distinction which must ever remain between Christ and the believer. We may copy Christ's life, but we can never equal it. His sinless life of infinite perfection may be faintly reflected by the saints. But His unique life cannot be duplicated. Waggoner's view of the final generation would make 144,000 little Christs. He said:

> When God has given this witness to the world of his power to save to the uttermost, to save sinful beings, and to live a perfect life in sinful flesh, then he will remove the disabilities and give us better circumstances in which to live. But first of all this wonder must be worked out in sinful man, not simply in the person of Jesus Christ, but in Jesus Christ reproduced and multiplied in the thousands of his followers. So that not simply in the few sporadic cases, but in the whole body of the church, the perfect life of Christ will be manifested to the world, and that will be the last crowning work which will either save or condemn men; and greater testimony than that there is not, and can not be, because there is none greater than God. When God is manifest among men, not simply as

---

35. Waggoner, "Sermon," *General Conference Bulletin* 4, no. 6, p. 148.
36. See Ellen G. White, *The Desire of Ages*, p. 466.

> God apart from man, but as God in man, suffering all that man suffered, subject to everything that man is subject to, what greater power can be manifested in the universe than that?[37]

This theology of reenactment is the spirit of antichrist. Christ's incarnation, life, death and resurrection are unique. They are unrepeatable events of salvation history. The church is called to rehearse these events—to re-present what has happened once and for all in Jesus Christ. But the church is never called to reenact the finished work of God in Jesus Christ.

In Waggoner's thinking, as in Romanism, the incarnation is extended throughout the church. It is then said we are not saved by faith in the historical acts of God in Christ but by a reenactment of these events in mystical experience. The historical Jesus merely serves as a Model of what God wants to do now and will do again in the final generation. One struggles in vain to find any real distinction between the sinless Christ and the final-generation saint. Waggoner was determined to remove all such distinctions. That is why he had to logically and inevitably go into pantheism.

Waggoner's *The Glad Tidings*

In 1900 the Pacific Press Publishing Association published Waggoner's commentary on Galatians under the title, *The Glad Tidings*. The material appeared originally as a series of articles in the *Signs of the Times* between November 24, 1898, and May 17, 1899. These articles on Galatians contained all the principal ingredi-

---

37. Waggoner, "Sermon," *General Conference Bulletin* 4, no. 17, p. 406.

ents of Waggoner's declining theology:

1. Justification was confounded with sanctification as in Roman Catholicism.[38]

2. An extreme sanctification had God or Christ or the Spirit doing the believing and obeying in and for the believer.[39]

3. It was said that Christ not only came in sinful flesh, but *is come* in sinful flesh—all sinful flesh.[40]

4. In a mystical view of the atonement, Christ was said to be crucified and risen in every man. A man only has to confess what is already a fact within him in order to be saved.[41]

5. *The Glad Tidings* was the product of a pantheistic theology.

---

38. "The meaning of the word 'justified' is 'made righteous.' This is the exact term that appears in other languages, which are not composed of foreign terms. The Latin word for righteousness is *justitia.* To be just is to be righteous. Then we add the termination *fy*, from the Latin word, meaning 'to make,' and we have the exact equivalent of the simpler term, 'make righteous'" (E. J. Waggoner, *The Glad Tidings*, 1900 ed., p. 77).

39. "Christ alone is righteous; He has overcome the world, and He alone has power to do it; in Him dwelleth all the fulness of God, because the law—God Himself—was in His heart; He alone has kept and can keep the law to perfection; therefore, only by His faith,—living faith, that is, His life in us,—can we be made righteous. . . .

"It follows, then, as a matter of course that, believing in Christ, we are justified by the faith of Christ, since we have Him personally dwelling in us, exercising His own faith. All power in heaven and earth is in His hands, and, recognizing this, we simply allow Him to exercise His own power in His own way" (ibid., pp. 80-81).

40. "To believe on His name means simply to believe that He dwells personally in every man,—in all flesh. We do not make it so by believing it; it is so, whether we believe it or not; we simply accept the fact, which all nature reveals to us" (ibid.).

41. "'Now that He ascended, what is it but that He also descended first into the lower parts of the earth?' Eph. 4:9. The risen Saviour is the crucified Saviour. As Christ risen is in the heart of the sinner, therefore, Christ crucified is there. If it were not so, there would be no hope for any. A man may

In 1972 the Pacific Press republished *The Glad Tidings* with a foreword by R. J. Wieland. The foreword and the comments on the book cover promote a dangerous myth about this book. They present *The Glad Tidings* as a true representation of the 1888 message with the theological endorsement of Ellen G. White. Wieland even makes the amazing claim that "the message of this book was in reality a transcript of studies that Dr. Waggoner gave personally to a gathering of ministers in Minneapolis, Minnesota, in the fall of 1888."[42]

The fact is that *The Glad Tidings* was written over ten years after 1888. There is a vast difference between Waggoner's theology in this book and the theology of his first treatise on Galatians written in 1887 in answer to

---

believe that Jesus was crucified eighteen hundred years ago, and may die in his sins; but he who believes that Christ is crucified and risen in him, has salvation.

"All that any man in the world has to do in order to be saved, is to believe the truth, that is, to recognize and acknowledge facts, to see things just as they actually are, and to confess them. Whoever believes that Christ is crucified in him, which is the fact in the case of every man, and confesses that the crucified Christ is also risen, and that He dwells in him by and with the power of the resurrection, is saved from sin, and will be saved as long as he holds fast his confession. This is the only true confession of faith.

"What a glorious thought that, wherever sin is, there is Christ, the Saviour from sin! He bears sin, all sin, the sin of the world. Sin is in all flesh, and so Christ is come in the flesh. Christ is crucified in every man that lives on earth. This is the word of truth, the Gospel of salvation, which is to be proclaimed to all, and which will save all who accept it. . . .

"He is not our substitute in the sense that one man is a substitute for another, in the army, for instance, the substitute being in one place, while the one for whom he is substitute is somewhere else, engaged in some other service. No; Christ's substitution is far different. He is our substitute in that He substitutes Himself for us, and we appear no more. We drop out entirely, so that it is 'not I, but Christ.' Thus we cast our cares on Him, not by picking them up and with an effort throwing them on Him, but by humbling ourselves into the nothingness that we are, so that we leave the burden resting on Him alone. Thus we see already how it is that He came" (ibid., pp. 87-8, 169).

42. Robert J. Wieland, Foreword to E. J. Waggoner, *The Glad Tidings*, 1972 ed.

Elder Butler and published in December, 1888. In 1888 Waggoner taught that justification was forensic. When he wrote *The Glad Tidings*, he had abandoned the Protestant doctrine entirely.

For Wieland to say *The Glad Tidings* reflects Waggoner's theology presented ten years earlier is bad enough. For him to claim it was a transcript of Waggoner's presentation in 1888 is even worse. There is no transcript of Waggoner's presentation at the conference of 1888. And Wieland has produced no evidence to support his claim that *The Glad Tidings* is an authentic representation of Waggoner's 1888 lectures. We protest the garbling of historical facts to support the tenuous claim that *The Glad Tidings* is an "Adventist Classic" containing the 1888 message endorsed by Ellen G. White.

Too many have failed to look objectively at Waggoner's history because they have theories of the incarnation, perfectionism and effective justification which coincide with his later teachings. They are really appealing to Waggoner, and through Waggoner to Ellen G. White, to support their theories. They are like the liberal Protestants and Roman Catholics now appealing to the early Luther of 1515-1516 for support in repudiating the Protestant doctrine of forensic justification.[43] The early Luther was a Roman Catholic not yet purged of his Catholic ideas on justification. It is a grievous error to project the theology of the early Luther into the teach-

---

43. See Lowell C. Green, "Faith, Righteousness and Justification: New Light on Their Development under Luther and Melanchthon," *Sixteenth Century Journal* 4, no. 1 (Apr. 1973): 65-86. Also deserving of careful study is Uuras Saarnivaara, *Luther Discovers the Gospel*. A weakness of this work, however, is its attempt to identify Luther's evangelical discovery with the problematic "tower experience." Green's article offers a more plausible solution.

ings of the mature Luther. Likewise, it is a monumental mistake for Adventists today to project the theology of the later Waggoner into the theology of the early Waggoner. It would be just as consistent for Wieland to take the pantheism of *The Glad Tidings* and project it back on the Waggoner of 1888.

Does Wieland realize that *The Glad Tidings* contains pantheism? Yes, in private correspondence he does.[44] And in preparing his revised edition of *The Glad Tidings* he editorially removed Waggoner's more blatant pantheistic statements.[45] In his foreword, however, Wieland gives no hint that he has done this.

By his editing Wieland implicitly admits we cannot project Waggoner's pantheism back to 1888. Then how does he know we can project Waggoner's views on effective or Roman Catholic justification, the sinful human nature of Christ and sanctification by faith alone back to 1888?

Careful historical investigation establishes a vast difference between Waggoner's theology of 1888 and his theology of 1898. Wieland cannot truly claim that Wag-

---

44. "Before I ever opened the cover of *The Glad Tidings* back in 1938, I had been warned by my teacher that there was pantheism in it" (Wieland to Lowell Tarling, 14 July 1977).

45. **Original 1900 Edition**

"To believe on His name is to believe that He is the Son of God; to believe that He is the Son of God, means to believe that He is come in the flesh, in human flesh, in our flesh, for His name is 'God with us;' so to believe on His name means simply to believe that He dwells personally in every man,—in all flesh. We do not make it so by believing it; it is so, whether we believe it or not; we simply accept the fact, which all nature reveals to us.

Edited 1972 Edition

"To believe on His name is to believe that He is the Son of God. To believe that He is the Son of God means to believe that He is come in the flesh, human flesh, our flesh. For His name is 'God with us.'

"So believing in Christ, we are justified by the faith of Christ, since we have Him personally dwelling in us, exercising His own faith. All power in heaven and earth is in His hands" (p. 42).

"It follows, then, as a matter of course that, believing in Christ, we are justified by the faith of Christ, since we have Him personally dwelling in us, exercising His own faith. All power in heaven and earth is in His hands" (pp. 80-81).

* * * * * * *

"Thorns are the sign of the curse, the weakened, imperfect condition of the earth (Gen. 3:17, 18; 4:11, 12); and on the cross Christ bore the crown of thorns. Therefore, all the curse, every trace of it, is borne by Christ,—by Christ crucified. Wherever, therefore, we see any curse, or wherever there is any curse, whether we see it or not, there is the cross of Christ. This can be seen again from the following: The curse is death, and death kills; the curse is in everything, yet everywhere we see life. Here is the miracle of the cross. Christ suffered the curse of death, and yet lived. He is the only one that could do it. Therefore, the fact that we see life everywhere, also in ourselves, in spite of the curse which is everywhere, is positive proof that the cross of the Crucified One is there bearing it. So it is that not only every blade of grass, every leaf of the forest, and every piece of bread that we eat has the stamp of the cross of Christ on it, but, above all, we have the same. Wherever there is a fallen, sin-scarred, miserable human being, there is also the Christ of God crucified for him and in him. Christ on the cross bears all things" (p. 85).

"Thorns are a sign of the curse (Genesis 3:17, 18), and Christ bore the crown of thorns. Every trace of the curse is borne by Christ.

"Wherever we see a fallen, sin-scarred, miserable human being, we ought to see also the Christ of God crucified for him. Christ on the cross bears all things" (p. 44).

* * * * * * *

"[Rom. 10:9 quoted.] What shall we confess about the Lord Jesus?—Why, confess the truth, that He is nigh thee, even in thy mouth and in thy heart, and believe that He is there risen from the dead. 'Now that He ascended, what is it but that He

"[Rom. 10:9 quoted.] What shall we confess about the Lord Jesus? Confess the truth, that He is near you, even in your mouth and in your heart, and believe that He is there risen from the dead. The risen Saviour is the crucified Saviour. As

also descended first into the lower parts of the earth?' Eph. 4:9. The risen Saviour is the crucified Saviour. As Christ risen is in the heart of the sinner, therefore, Christ crucified is there. If it were not so, there would be no hope for any. A man may believe that Jesus was crucified eighteen hundred years ago, and may die in his sins; but he who believes that Christ is crucified and risen in him, has salvation.

"All that any man in the world has to do in order to be saved, is to believe the truth, that is, to recognize and acknowledge facts, to see things just as they actually are, and to confess them. Whoever believes that Christ is crucified in him, which is the fact in the case of every man, and confesses that the crucified Christ is also risen, and that He dwells in him by and with the power of the resurrection, is saved from sin, and will be saved as long as he holds fast his confession. This is the only true confession of faith.

"What a glorious thought that, wherever sin is, there is Christ, the Saviour from sin! He bears sin, all sin, the sin of the world. Sin is in all flesh, and so Christ is come in the flesh. Christ is crucified in every man that lives on earth. This is the word of truth, the Gospel of salvation, which is to be proclaimed to all, and which will save all who accept it" (pp. 87-8).

Christ risen is in the heart of the sinner, therefore Christ crucified is there. If it were not so, there would be no hope for any. A man may believe that Jesus was crucified two millennia ago, and may die in his sins. But he who believes that Christ is crucified and risen in him has salvation.

"All any man in the world has to do in order to be saved is to believe the truth; that is, to recognize and acknowledge facts, to see things just as they actually are, and to confess them. Whoever believes that Christ is crucified in him, risen in him, and dwells in him, is saved from sin. And he will be saved as long as he holds to his belief. This is the only true confession of faith" (p. 45).

* * * * * * *

"Note that our sins were 'in His body.' It was no superficial work that He undertook. The sins were not merely figuratively laid on Him, but they were actually in Him. He was made a curse for us, made to be sin for us, and consequently suffered death for us.

"To some this truth seems repugnant" (p. 117).

"Note that our sins were '*in His body*.' It was no superficial work that He undertook. Our sins were not merely figuratively laid on Him, but were 'in His body.' He was 'made a curse' for us, 'made to be sin' for us, and consequently suffered death for us.

"To some this truth seems repugnant" (p. 62).

goner's pantheism in *The Glad Tidings* was only a parasite rather than a vital and inherent part of his basic understanding of righteousness by faith.[46] We believe we have clearly demonstrated that Waggoner's thinking on justification, sanctification, the atonement and the incarnation was integral to his pantheism. Moreover, historical theology proves that the ideas Waggoner taught in all these areas logically lead to pantheism. His theology of 1898-1899 was so thoroughly contaminated that nothing could possibly be salvaged from it. Yet the Pacific Press presents it today as though it contained the holy delicacies of 1888 itself.

* * * * * * *

"[2 Cor. 5:21, R.V. quoted.] In the fullest sense of the word, and to a degree that is seldom thought of when the expression is used, He became man's substitute. That is, He permeates our being, identifying Himself so fully with us that everything that touches or affects us touches and affects Him. He is not our substitute in the sense that one man is a substitute for another, in the army, for instance, the substitute being in one place, while the one for whom he is substitute is somewhere else, engaged in some other service. No; Christ's substitution is far different. He is our substitute in that He substitutes Himself for us, and we appear no more. We drop out entirely, so that it is 'not I, but Christ.' Thus we cast our cares on Him, not by picking them up and with an effort throwing them on Him, but by humbling ourselves into the nothingness that we are, so that we leave the burden resting on Him alone" (p. 169).

"[2 Cor. 5:21, R.V. quoted.]

"In the fullest sense of the word and to a degree seldom thought of when the expression is used, He became man's substitute. That is, He identifies Himself so fully with us that everything that touches or affects us, touches and affects Him. 'Not I, but Christ.' We cast our cares on Him by humbling ourselves into the nothingness that we are and leaving our burden on Him alone" (p. 91).

46. "The pantheism was not inherent in his understanding of RbF [righteousness by faith], but a parasite. Hence I wished to restore the message as nearly as I could to its original purity as he gave it in the early 1888 era" (Wieland to Tarling, 14 July 1977).

Wieland is not alone in this historical misunderstanding of Waggoner. The myth extends to men like A. G. Daniells, who commended E. J. Waggoner's book, *The Everlasting Covenant*, as one which would "place a flood of light in the homes of our people."[47] Furthermore, *The Glad Tidings* had to pass official editorial inspection in 1900. So Wieland is not the only one who could see little wrong and much to laud in the book.

Waggoner's *The Everlasting Covenant*

In 1900 the International Tract Society, a Seventh-day Adventist publishing house in London, published Waggoner's largest work, *The Everlasting Covenant*. Most of the book first appeared as a series of articles in the British *Present Truth*, beginning in May, 1896. In some respects it was the later Waggoner's best work. It dealt largely with gospel lessons from Abraham and the history of Israel. Waggoner's concept of the unity of God's covenant was probably a first in Adventist literature. It did not forcefully appear again until Dr. Edward Heppenstall's work on the one everlasting covenant in the 1950's.[48]

Waggoner's work, however, was thoroughly marred by pantheism. He repeated in great detail his pantheistic ideas on the life of Christ in all creation and in all men.[49] He declared that ordinary bread is the real body of

---

47. A. V. Olson, *Through Crisis to Victory: 1888-1901*, p. 231.

48. Edward Heppenstall, "The Covenants and the Law," in *Our Firm Foundation*, 1:435-92.

49. E. J. Waggoner, *The Everlasting Covenant*, pp. 247-49.

Christ[50] and that the real presence of Christ is in ordinary water.[51] He spiritualized the temple of God "in heaven" and said it is composed of living people.[52] Of course, this involved an understanding of "the cleansing of the sanctuary" entirely contrary to historic Adventism.[53] Waggoner also repeated Westcott's theory of the mystical atonement.[54]

The Everlasting Covenant is devoid of the great biblical and Protestant doctrine of forensic justification—a salvation by imputation, representation and substitution. Salvation is reduced to a purely subjective process. The book is entirely consistent with the other material of Waggoner's declining years.

One statement in *The Everlasting Covenant* should be familiar to those acquainted with certain concepts taught in Adventism in the 1970's. It expresses Waggoner's perfectionism relating to the final generation. He said:

> Before the end comes, and at the time of the coming of Christ, there must be a people on earth, not necessarily large in proportion to the number of inhabitants of earth, but large enough to be known in all the earth, in whom "all the fulness of God" will be manifest even as it was in Jesus of Nazareth. God will demonstrate to the world that what he did with Jesus of Nazareth He can do with anyone who will yield to Him.[55]

This was directly related to Waggoner's view that Christ came in sinful human nature. So he could say,

---

50. Ibid., pp. 254-59.
51. Ibid., pp. 262-70.
52. Ibid., pp. 357-64.
53. Waggoner, *Confession of Faith*, pp. 14-15.
54. Waggoner, *Everlasting Covenant*, p. 365.
55. Ibid., p. 366.

"The Lord wants all to understand that the new birth puts men in the same position that Christ occupied on this earth, and He will demonstrate this before the world."[56]

In his book, *Through Crisis to Victory*, A. V. Olson quotes from a letter written by A. G. Daniells to W. C. White on May 12, 1902. In this letter Daniells stated: "I am deeply convinced that something ought to be done to place a flood of light in the homes of our people. I know of no better book to do this, outside of the Bible, than Brother Waggoner's book."[57]

It is uncertain whether Daniells was referring to Waggoner's *The Glad Tidings* or to his book, *The Everlasting Covenant*, since both were published about this time. Olson assumes Daniells was referring to *The Everlasting Covenant* since the covenants were an issue at that time. Olson, however, wrongly ascribes its authorship to J. H. Waggoner, E. J. Waggoner's father. Apparently Olson overlooked the evidence that *The Glad Tidings* was the work to which Daniells referred in his letter to W. C. White.

Early in 1902 three articles by William Brickley appeared in the *Review and Herald*. These articles upheld the view that the ceremonial law was the law that Paul considered in the book of Galatians. This view created some agitation. Writing to Butler on April 11, 1902, Daniells stated that these articles, published with Uriah Smith's approval, "were openly and squarely against the message that came to this people at Minneapolis and that has been embraced by thousands of our people and openly and repeatedly endorsed by the Spirit of prophecy. These articles," he continued, "have caused a great

---

56. Ibid., p. 367.

57. Olson, *Crisis to Victory*, p. 231.

deal of trouble and dissatisfaction among our brethren in different States."[58]

For our present purposes it matters little whether Daniells was referring to *The Glad Tidings* or *The Everlasting Covenant.* It is disturbing, however, that either of Waggoner's works should have received unqualified endorsement by such leading brethren.

Waggoner's View of the Blotting Out of Sin

On September 30, 1902, the *Review and Herald* published Waggoner's article entitled "The Blotting Out of Sin."[59] In recent years this article has often been cited by those holding views similar to Waggoner's.

Waggoner's article is consistent with the tenor of his later theological thinking. It shows he had entirely lost the forensic categories of biblical thought. Like a Roman Catholic, he regarded sin primarily as a disease. He said sin is blotted out by being erased from the nature. Waggoner had lost the true Protestant faith that views sin primarily as guilt. Guilt is not erased by inner renewal. It is a legal debt. It can be erased only by Christ's substitutionary death and the application of the merits of that blood by the high-priestly intercession of Christ.

But Waggoner made no distinction between the work of the interceding priest in heaven and the work of the Spirit in the heart. Mediatorial cleansing by blood is instantaneous and complete, for it is a judicial cleansing (1 John 1:9) done *for* the believing sinner. This is justifica-

---

58. Ibid., p. 230.

59. E. J. Waggoner, "The Blotting Out of Sin," *Review and Herald*, 30 Sept. 1902, p. 8.

tion. The cleansing of the Holy Spirit is a process which begins at conversion. This is sanctification, which is never complete until glorification.

Waggoner's statement on the blotting out of sins significantly illustrates that blurring the distinction between justification and sanctification leads to blurring the distinction between the Creator and the creature. That is to say, it leads to pantheism. Waggoner wrote:

> Truth is implanted in the heavens and earth; it fills the stars, and keeps them in their places; it is that by which the plants grow, and the birds build their nests; it is that by which they know how to find their way across the sea. When Moses broke the tables of stone, the law was just as steadfast as it was before. Just so, though all the record of all our sin, even though written with the finger of God, were erased, the sin would remain, because the sin is in us. Though the record of our sin were graven in the rock, and the rock should be ground to powder,—even this would not blot out our sin.[60]

The Closing Years

In 1903 Mrs. White expressed the hope that Waggoner would escape the snare of pantheism and regain his former power. There is no evidence he did so. Neither theology nor human life can be in harmony with God unless it preserves the distinctions ordained by God. One of the vital distinctions in human existence is the distinction between male and female. And along with that, there is the distinction between a man's relationship to his wife and all other women. Tragically, Waggoner lost that distinction too.

When Waggoner attended the General Conference of

60. Ibid.

1901, he apparently voiced certain views on "spiritual affinity" which he had espoused earlier in Great Britain. In essence these views stated that although one is not rightfully a marriage partner in this life, a present spiritual union is allowed on the basis that he or she might be married in the life to come. Later, in 1908, Ellen G. White called these views "dangerous, misleading fables" she had been forced to confront following 1844. She clearly recognized that "Dr. Waggoner was then departing from the faith in the doctrine he held regarding spiritual affinities."[61]

We do not sit in judgment on Waggoner's character or destiny. To his credit he behaved himself like a gentleman in the face of bitter opposition. He never showed bitterness against the church or his former brethren. Waggoner appeared to be a humble man, and his last *Confession* is written in the spirit of a Christian believer. His faith was certainly not perfect, but we fondly believe he died trusting in a perfect Saviour. If that be the case, Waggoner's decline was not the end of the story. Although his great enemy must have rejoiced at his fall, that fall was not the final end. "Do not gloat over me, my enemy! Though I have fallen, I will rise" (Micah 7:8, NIV).

---

61. Ellen G. White, Letter 224, 1908; cited in Olson, *Crisis to Victory*, p. 313.

10

Waggoner in Retrospect

E. J. Waggoner's theological development is not a matter of mere historical interest. The issue of righteousness by faith and the drama of 1888 have regained great prominence in the Seventh-day Adventist community. Not surprisingly, some of Waggoner's works have been republished. His name is being invoked in support of various theories now promoted within the church. And the works of Waggoner the pantheist are extolled as though they represented the precious light of 1888 which had Ellen G. White's full endorsement.

We believe we have amply demonstrated that Waggoner's pantheism was not a theological aberration isolated from the rest of his theological system. His mind was too orderly and logical for that. His premises on justification by faith, sanctification, the human nature of Christ and the mystical atonement logically lead to pantheism. The best historical theology confirms this. And Waggoner himself has proved it true. His history clearly demonstrates where such ideas as "effective" justification, sanctification by faith alone, the sinful nature of Christ, perfectionism and the mystical atonement lead. If we refuse to learn the lessons of history, we shall be condemned to repeat them.

The Waggoner who abandoned the Protestant doctrine of justification by faith after 1888 and finally espoused "the alpha of deadly heresies" is alive and well represented in Adventism today.

Justification

The fatal flaw in Waggoner's theology was his failure to guard cardinal distinctions which must be preserved if we are to avoid confusing God and man. The first vital distinction Waggoner lost was the clear distinction between justification and sanctification—God's work *for* us and His work *in* us. Of course, there is also a vital union between the two. But we must not argue from their union to make a fusion. Adventism's stress on the union of law and gospel has always made her prone to blur the vital distinction between law and gospel.

Losing the distinction between the righteousness of faith and sanctification corrupted Waggoner's understanding of both. He could no longer stand with the Reformers, who clearly grasped that the righteousness of faith—Christ's personal obedience alone—is a righteousness unspoiled by any human participation. Whereas the righteousness of faith is wholly substitutionary, sanctification involves man's active response to God in a life of willing obedience and is therefore not by faith alone.

The Bible does not call sanctification "God's righteousness" or "the righteousness of faith" but rather "our righteousness," "his [the believer's] righteousness" or "the righteousness of the law." Though performed in the strength given him of God, this righteousness of the believer is never perfect in this life. It is never entirely free from the contamination of sinful human nature. While good works testify to the genuineness of the believer's faith, they cannot satisfy the demands of God's law unless Christ's merit is added to them. The believer cannot stand in the judgment because of this active righteousness, although he will not stand without it. Furthermore, no one who confuses this active righteousness—sanctification—with the righteousness of faith can stand before God with a good conscience because he would be trusting in that which is incomplete and imperfect for his salvation.

This relationship between righteousness by faith and sanctification is one of the principal points in the current discussion on righteousness by faith. Some insist that the righteousness of the born-again believer is part of "the righteousness of faith" which Paul considers in the book of Romans. And some appeal to Waggoner to support their mingling of these two kinds of righteousness.

A related approach which blurs the distinction between justification and sanctification is the old theory of "effective" justification.[1] If proponents of effective justification simply meant that justification always has sanctifying effects, they would reflect the best Protestant heritage. But the theory of effective justification has a definite history and is therefore very suspect. In the sixteenth century *justum efficere* was the term used by Roman Catholic apologists who contended that "to justify" means "to make righteous" in a subjective sense. Thus the Romanists confounded justification and sanctification. Around the beginning of this century a number of theologians wanted to discard the Protestant

---

1. See Hans K. LaRondelle, "The Shaking of Adventism? IV; Paxton and the Reformers," *Spectrum* 9, no. 3 (July 1978): 45-57.

concept of forensic justification by remodeling Luther. They used terms like "analytical justification," "sanative justification" and finally "effective justification." In every instance they infused sanctification into the article of justification so that the true Protestant doctrine was lost. The theory of effective justification blurs the distinction between justification and sanctification, thus corrupting both. Carried to its logical end, it destroys the vital distinction between God's work and man's work. It puts man where God alone should be, and God where man should be.

Some within Adventism do not hesitate to say justification is an internal "making righteous."[2] They follow Roman Catholicism, which confuses justification with sanctification. The post-1888 Waggoner is clearly alive and well in Adventism today.

Sanctification

The saving righteousness for which Paul so earnestly contends is "by faith alone." Those who confound this article with sanctification inevitably contend for sanctification by faith alone.[3] They say that God—Christ or the Holy Spirit—so lives in the believer that He alone does all the believing, working and obeying. The believer passively permits the Deity to do everything in him.

This is quietism. It fails to do justice to the meaningful activity of the believer. It tends to be effeminate and mystical in its view of the Christian life. It lacks the robust virility of biblical Christianity, which sets the

2. See Erwin R. Gane, "Is There Power in Justification?" See also A. John Clifford and Russell R. Standish, *Conflicting Concepts of Righteousness by Faith in the Seventh-day Adventist Church: Australasian Division.*

3. See Morris L. Venden, *Salvation by Faith and Your Will.*

justified believer free for legitimate work because his work is no longer done on his own account. Passive sanctification is also generally perfectionistic. If Christ alone does the work for and in the believer, that work is considered perfect and sometimes meritorious.

Sanctification by faith alone tends to pantheism because it blurs the distinction between the work of the Creator and the work of the creature. This was Waggoner's theory of sanctification when he lost the Protestant doctrine of forensic justification. And who would deny that this Waggoner is alive and well in Adventism today?

For years so-called exponents of righteousness by faith have reflected the "victorious-life" theories of the holiness movement. But when Paul and the Reformers spoke of righteousness by faith, they were not referring to some experience of inner piety. They were referring to that infinite, awesome and unrepeatable event when God acted in Christ for man's redemption. This event was historical, juridical and objective. To the apostles and Reformers the gospel was the announcement of this great act of God in Christ. It was faith in God's act which set men free—free from themselves and from their preoccupation with obtaining enough internal piety to stand in the judgment of God. There is nothing more pitiful nor more destructive of true holiness than the Waggonerian tendency to internalize the righteousness of faith.

The Incarnation

Waggoner's doctrine of the sinful human nature of Christ played a conspicuous role in his developing pantheism. With the publication of *Questions on Doctrine* in 1957, it appeared that this doctrine of the sinful human nature of Christ had been expelled from Adventism. But it is no secret that some church leaders have tried to revive the theory of the sinful human nature of Christ.[4] They believe this view was part of the 1888 message which enjoyed Ellen G. White's support. And they are consequently agitating Waggoner's doctrine on the sinful human nature of Christ and the incarnation.

Perfectionism

Waggoner's extreme view on sanctification—that Christ actually thinks and obeys in the believer—and his theory on the incarnation were in harmony with his perfectionism. He taught that Christ lived in sinful human nature two thousand years ago to prove He can do it again in the believer today. In this theology the incarnation is no longer absolutely unique. It continues happening all the time. Rome taught that the church was the extension of the incarnation. Waggoner proposed that the believer is an extension of the incarnation. The following statement by Waggoner the pantheist in 1903 was quoted approvingly in a recent *Review* editorial.

> From the manger in Bethlehem shine the rays that shall fill the earth with the glory of the Lord; and that coming glory will be hastened as the manger is multiplied by the repetition of the mystery of the birth of Christ in all who receive him.[5]

---

4. See Herbert E. Douglass, "The Humanity of the Son of God Is Everything to Us," *Review and Herald*, 23 Dec. 1971, pp. 12-13; idem, "Jesus Showed Us the Possible," ibid., 30 Dec. 1971, pp. 16-17; idem, "The Demonstration That Settles Everything," ibid., 6 Jan. 1972, pp. 13-14; idem, "Men of Faith—The Showcase of God's Grace," in Herbert E. Douglass, Edward Heppenstall, Hans K. LaRondelle and C. Mervyn Maxwell, *Perfection: The Impossible Possibility*, pp. 13-56.

5. E. J. Waggoner, "The Manger and the Cross," *Review and Herald*, 6 Jan. 1903, p. 9. Cf. Kenneth H. Wood, "Christmas 1976," *Review and Herald*, 23 Dec. 1976, p. 2.

During the 1974 North American Bible Conferences, Herbert E. Douglass presented his thesis on the perfection of the final generation. Significantly, he supported his position by quoting Waggoner's lectures of 1897—lectures permeated with pantheism.[6] In recent years Douglass has been a leading exponent of Waggoner's final-generation concept. He has presented this in *Review* editorials, the North American Bible Conferences, the Adult Sabbath School Lesson Quarterly on *Jesus, the Model Man* and in the books, *Why Jesus Waits* and *Jesus, the Benchmark of Humanity*. These are all echoes of the perfectionism of Waggoner, who said:

> Before the end comes, and at the time of the coming of Christ, there must be a people on earth, not necessarily large in proportion to the number of inhabitants of earth, but large enough to be known in all the earth, in whom "all the fulness of God" will be manifest even as it was in Jesus of Nazareth. God will demonstrate to the world that what he did with Jesus of Nazareth He can do with anyone who will yield to Him.[7]

The Atonement

Waggoner's mystical theory of atonement is also alive and well in Adventism today. The tendency to dissipate the biblical concept of the wrath of God and the propitiatory death of Christ have been present in certain quarters for at least thirty years. Robert J. Wieland embraces Waggoner's view that Christ's death did not propitiate God's wrath but man's enmity. The connection between the doctrine of the sinful human nature of Christ and the mystical atonement is well known in the

---

6. Herbert E. Douglass, "The Unique Contribution of Adventist Eschatology."

7. E. J. Waggoner, *The Everlasting Covenant*, p. 366.

history of Christian thought. Berkhof wrote:

> The mystical theory has this in common with the moral influence theory, that it conceives of the atonement exclusively as exercising influence on man and bringing about a change in him. At the same time it differs from the moral influence theory in that it conceives of the change wrought in man, not primarily as an ethical change in the conscious life of man, but a deeper change in the subconscious life which is brought about in a mystical way. The basic principle of this theory is that, in the incarnation, the divine life entered into the life of humanity, in order to lift it to the plane of the divine. Christ possessed human nature with its inborn corruption and predisposition to moral evil; but through the influence of the Holy Spirit He was kept from manifesting this corruption in actual sin, gradually purified human nature, and in His death completely extirpated this original depravity and reunited that nature to God. He entered the life of mankind as a transforming leaven, and the resulting transformation constitutes His redemption. This is in effect, though with differences of detail, the theory of Schleiermacher, Edward Irving, Menken, and Stier. Even Kohlbruegge seemed inclined to accept it in a measure. It is burdened, however, with the following difficulties:
>
> 1. It takes no account of the guilt of man. According to Scripture the guilt of man must be removed, in order that he may be purified of his pollution; but the mystical theory, disregarding the guilt of sin, concerns itself only with the expulsion of the pollution of sin. It knows of no justification, and conceives of salvation as consisting in subjective sanctification.
>
> 2. It rests upon false principles, where it finds in the natural order of the universe an exhaustive expression of the will and nature of God, regards sin exclusively as a power of moral evil in the world, which involves no guilt and deserves no punishment, and looks upon punishment as a mere reaction of the law of the universe against the transgressor, and not at all as a revelation of the personal wrath of God against sin.

> 3. It contradicts Scripture where it makes Christ share in the pollution of sin and hereditary depravity, and deduces the necessity of His death from the sinfulness of His own nature (not all do this). By doing this, it makes it impossible to regard Him as the sinless Saviour who, just because of His sinlessness, could take the place of sinners and pay the penalty for them.
>
> 4. It has no answer to the question, how those who lived before the incarnation can share in the redemption of Jesus Christ. If Christ in some realistic way drove out the pollution of sin during the time of His sojourn on earth, and now continues to drive it out; and if the salvation of man depends on this subjective process, how then could the Old Testament saints share in this salvation?[8]

Berkhof has essentially described Waggoner's teaching on the atonement in the 1890's. Berkhof's description also has a close bearing on Wieland's theology.

But the most remarkable revival of Waggonerian-like views on the atonement has taken place in the Division of Religion at Loma Linda University. In this department are those who repudiate the historic Christian doctrine of the substitutionary atonement in order to embrace "the moral influence theory." In fact, the moral influence theory has widely permeated West-Coast American Adventism. It has such a stranglehold on the church's principal financial base that the leaders of the church appear paralyzed and frightened to touch it.

A. Graham Maxwell's recent denominational book of the year, *Can God Be Trusted?* is conspicuous for what it omits in discussing the atonement. The chapter, "Why Did Jesus Have to Die?" should be compared with an article of similar title written by Waggoner in the British *Present Truth* of September 21, 1893.[9]

---

8. Louis Berkhof, *Systematic Theology*, pp. 389-90.

9. E. J. Waggoner, "Why Did Christ Die?" *Present Truth*, 21 Sept. 1893, pp. 385-88. Cf. A. Graham Maxwell, *Can God Be Trusted?* pp. 75-89.

Summary

Confounding justification with sanctification, extreme views of sanctification, the doctrine of the sinful human nature of Christ, the mystical atonement and the repudiation of the legal categories of biblical thought all lead logically to a pantheistic theology. Church history in general testifies to this. Adventist history also demonstrates this. We have seen that all the major tenets of Waggoner's post-1888 theology have been revived in Adventism today. Where will these views lead? We do not have to speculate.

If the proper distinction between the saving righteousness of faith and the consequent righteousness of the believer is lost, all is lost. To use Luther's words, "nothing remains but darkness and ignorance of God." Such great objective truths as the incarnation, the atonement and justification cannot be internalized and dehistoricized without prostituting the Christian faith.

But we end on an optimistic note. The Waggoner of 1884-1888 has also been revived and lives in Adventism today. This is the Waggoner who was committed to restoring the Reformation message of justification by the imputed righteousness of Jesus Christ. Those who now stand in this stream of thought can also profit by Waggoner's history.

Selective Bibliography

General Bibliography

Andrews, J. N. "Christ and the Law." *Signs of the Times*, 23 Sept. 1886, p. 582.

———. Reply to H. E. Carver. *Review and Herald*, 16 Sept. 1851, p. 29.

———. "Watchman, What of the Night?" *Review and Herald*, 27 May 1852, p. 15.

Berkhof, Louis. *Systematic Theology*. 4th revised and enlarged ed. Grand Rapids: Wm. B. Eerdmans Publishing Co., 1941.

Boettner, Loraine. *Studies in Theology*. 13th ed. Grand Rapids: Baker Book House, 1975.

Brickley, William. "Notes on the Book of Galatians." Nos. 1-3. *Review and Herald*, 21 Jan. 1902; 28 Jan. 1902, p. 52; 4 Feb. 1902, p. 67.

Brown, Robert McAfee. *The Spirit of Protestantism*. London: Oxford University Press, 1965.

Buchanan, James. *The Doctrine of Justification: An Outline of Its History in the Church and of Its Exposition from Scripture*. Reprint. Grand Rapids: Baker Book House, 1977.

Bunyan, John. *The Riches of Bunyan.* New York: American Tract Society, 1850.

Butler, George I. *The Law in the Book of Galatians: Is It the Moral Law, or Does It Refer to that System of Laws Peculiarly Jewish?* Battle Creek, Mich.: Review & Herald Publishing House, 1886.

———. "Laws Which Are 'Contrary to Us,' a 'Yoke of Bondage,' and 'Not Good.'" *Review and Herald*, 22 Mar. 1887.

———. "Our Righteousness vs. Christ's Righteousness." *Review and Herald*, 23 Sept. 1884.

Carpenter, George L. "Sketches from the Life of Ellet Joseph Waggoner (Jan. 12, 1855–May 28, 1916)." A paper presented in partial fulfillment of the requirements for the course CH570, History of the Seventh-day Adventist Church, Andrews University, May, 1973.

Chemnitz, Martin. *Examination of the Council of Trent*, Part 1. Translated by Fred Kramer. St. Louis: Concordia Publishing House, 1971.

Christian, Lewis H. *The Fruitage of Spiritual Gifts: The Influence and Guidance of Ellen G. White in the Advent Movement.* Washington, D.C.: Review & Herald Publishing Assn., 1947.

"Christ Our Righteousness." *Review and Herald*, 27 May 1976, pp. 4-7. A joint statement of the Palmdale, California, conference on righteousness by faith, April 23-30, 1976.

Clifford, A. John, and Standish, Russell R. *Conflicting Concepts of Righteousness by Faith in the Seventh-day Adventist Church: Australasian Division.* Victoria, Australia: published by the authors, 1976. Biblical Research Institute paper.

Cramp, J. M. *The Council of Trent.* London: Religious Tract Society, 1840.

Daily Bulletin of the General Conference 8 (1899).

Daniells, Arthur G. *Christ Our Righteousness*. Washington, D.C.: Review & Herald Publishing Assn., 1941.

Dillenberger, John, ed. *Martin Luther: Selections from His Writings*. Garden City, N.Y.: Anchor Books, 1961.

Douglass, Herbert E. "The Demonstration That Settles Everything." *Review and Herald*, 6 Jan. 1972, pp. 13-14.

———. "The Humanity of the Son of God Is Everything to Us." *Review and Herald*, 23 Dec. 1971, pp. 12-13.

———. "Jesus Showed Us the Possible." *Review and Herald*, 30 Dec. 1971, pp. 16-17.

———. *Jesus, the Model Man*. Adult Sabbath School Lesson Quarterly, April-June 1977. Warburton, Vict., Australia: Signs Publishing Co., 1977.

———. "Men of Faith—The Showcase of God's Grace." In Herbert E. Douglass, Edward Heppenstall, Hans K. LaRondelle and C. Mervyn Maxwell, *Perfection: The Impossible Possibility*. Nashville: Southern Publishing Assn., 1975.

———. "The Unique Contribution of Adventist Eschatology." In *North American Bible Conference, 1974*, edited by the Biblical Research Committee of the General Conference. Washington, D.C.: General Conference of Seventh-day Adventists, 1974. A paper presented at the 1974 North American Division Bible conferences.

———. *Why Jesus Waits*. Washington, D.C.: Review & Herald Publishing Assn., 1976.

———, and Van Dolson, Leo R. *Jesus, the Benchmark of Humanity*. Nashville: Southern Publishing Assn., 1976.

Ford, J. O., comp. *Lessons on Faith: A Selection of Articles and Sermons by A. T. Jones and E. J. Waggoner*. Calistoga, Calif.: John O. Ford, M.D., 1977.

Froom, LeRoy E. *Movement of Destiny*. Washington, D.C.: Review & Herald Publishing Assn., 1971.

Gane, Erwin R. "The Arian or Anti-Trinitarian Views Presented in Seventh-day Adventist Literature and the Ellen G. White Answer." Master's thesis, Andrews University, 1963.

———. "Is There Power in Justification?" Mimeographed. Angwin, Calif.: Pacific Union College, n.d. [c. 1977].

General Conference Daily Bulletin 2 (1888).

Green, Lowell C. "Faith, Righteousness and Justification: New Light on Their Development Under Luther and Melanchthon." *Sixteenth Century Journal* 4, no. 1 (Apr. 1973): 36-57.

———. "Luther Research in English-Speaking Countries Since 1971." *Lutherjahrbuch* 44 (1977).

Haddock, Robert. "A History of the Doctrine of the Sanctuary in the Advent Movement: 1800-1905." B.D. thesis, Andrews University, 1970.

Heppenstall, Edward. "The Covenants and the Law." In *Our Firm Foundation*, vol. 1. Washington, D.C.: Review & Herald Publishing Assn., 1953.

Hoeksema, Herman. *Reformed Dogmatics*. Grand Rapids: Reformed Free Publishing Assn., 1966.

Howard, Pearl Waggoner. "Biographical Sketch and Background." N.p., n.d. A biographical sketch of E. J. Waggoner by his daughter.

Hudson, A. L., ed. *A Warning and Its Reception*. Baker, Oreg.: Hudson Printing Co., n.d. [c. 1960].

Hughes, Thomas H. *The Atonement: Modern Theories of the Doctrine*. London: George Allen & Unwin, 1949.

Hyde, Gordon M. "Righteousness by Faith Symposium in Washington." *Ministry*, Oct. 1978, p. 13. A brief summary of the Righteousness by Faith Symposium, held in Washington, D.C., August 6-11, 1978.

Jones, A. T. Letter to Claude Holmes. 12 May 1921. Washington, D.C. Ellen G. White Estate. D. File 189.

LaRondelle, Hans K. "The Shaking of Adventism? IV; Paxton and the Reformers." *Spectrum* 9, no. 3 (July 1978): 45-57.

Luther, Martin. *A Commentary on St. Paul's Epistle to the Galatians*. Cambridge: James Clarke & Co., 1953. Prepared by Philip S. Watson, this is a revised and completed translation based on the "Middleton" edition of the English version of 1575.

———. *Luther's Works*. American ed. St. Louis: Concordia Publishing House; Philadelphia: Muhlenberg Press, 1955-1975. Vols. 26, 27, *Lectures on Galatians—1535*, edited and translated by Jaroslav Pelikan, 1963, 1964. Vol. 34, *Career of the Reformer: IV*, edited by Lewis W. Spitz, 1960.

Maxwell, A. Graham. *Can God Be Trusted?* Nashville: Southern Publishing Assn., 1977.

McReynolds, C. "Experiences While at the General Conference in Minneapolis, Minn., in 1888." Washington, D.C. Ellen G. White Estate. D. File 189. Mimeographed.

Morris, Leon. *The Apostolic Preaching of the Cross*. 3rd ed. London: Tyndale Press, 1965.

Moxom, Philip S. "Christ 'the End of the Law.'" *Signs of the Times*, 5 June 1884, pp. 338-39.

Nash, R. T. "An Eye Witness Account." In letter to Ellen G. White Estate, 25 June 1955. Mimeographed.

———. *An Eyewitness Report of the 1888 General Conference at Minneapolis of Seventh-day Adventists*. Highland, Calif.: published by the author, n.d.

———. "Memories of Minneapolis." Letter to Arthur L. White, Ellen G. White Estate, 9 July 1955.

New Schaff-Herzog Encyclopedia of Religious Knowledge, The. 15 vols. Reprint. Grand Rapids: Baker Book House, 1977.

Olson, A. V. *Through Crisis to Victory: 1888-1901*. Washington, D.C.: Review & Herald Publishing Assn., 1966.

Pearce, David. "Your Bible Says This About—The Three Angels' Messages." *Signs of the Times*, Aug. 1978, pp. 6-7.

Pease, Norval F. *By Faith Alone*. Mountain View, Calif.: Pacific Press Publishing Assn., 1962.

———. "The Faith That Saves." Nos. 1-6. *Review and Herald*, 21 Aug. 1969, pp. 4-5; 28 Aug. 1969, pp. 2-4; 4 Sept. 1969, pp. 2-3; 11 Sept. 1969, pp. 5-7; 18 Sept. 1969, pp. 5-7; 25 Sept. 1969, pp. 5-6.

———. "Justification and Righteousness by Faith in the Seventh-day Adventist Church before 1900." Masters thesis, Seventh-day Adventist Theological Seminary, 1945.

Rendalen, Age. "The Nature and Extent of Ellen White's Endorsement of Waggoner and Jones." A paper presented in partial fulfillment of the requirements for the course GREL610, Research Methods, and CHIS574, Development of Seventh-day Adventist Theology, Andrews University, School of Graduate Studies, December, 1978.

"Righteousness-by-Faith Report." *Ministry*, Aug. 1976, pp. 6-9. Report of the Righteousness by Faith Committee, which met February, 1975, in Takoma Park, Maryland.

Robinson, Dores. Letter to W. H. Branson. 8 May 1935.

———. *The Story of Our Health Message*. 3rd ed., revised and enlarged. Nashville: Southern Publishing Assn., 1965.

Robinson, William C. *The Reformation: A Rediscovery of Grace*. Grand Rapids: Wm. B. Eerdmans Publishing Co., 1962.

Ryle, J. C. *Holiness*. London: James Clarke & Co., 1956.

Saarnivaara, Uuras. Luther Discovers the Gospel. St. Louis: Concordia Publishing House, 1951.

Schaff, Philip. *History of the Christian Church*. 2nd ed., rev. 8 vols. 1910. Reprint. Grand Rapids: Wm. B. Eerdmans Publishing Co., 1974.

Seventh-day Adventist Bible Commentary, The. Edited by Francis D. Nichol. Commentary Reference Series, vols. 1-7. Washington, D.C.: Review & Herald Publishing Assn., 1952-1957.

Seventh-day Adventist Encyclopedia. Edited by Don F. Neufeld. Commentary Reference Series, vol. 10. Rev. ed. Washington, D.C.: Review & Herald Publishing Assn., 1976.

Seventh-day Adventists Answer Questions on Doctrine. Washington, D.C.: Review & Herald Publishing Assn., 1957. "Prepared by a Representative Group of Seventh-day Adventist Leaders, Bible Teachers, and Editors."

Seventh-day Adventist Year Book, The. Battle Creek, Mich.: Review & Herald Publishing House, 1887.

Smith, Uriah. Letter to Ellen G. White. 17 Feb. 1890.

———. "Our Righteousness." *Review and Herald*, 11 June 1889.

———. "Our Righteousness Again." *Review and Herald*, 2 July 1889.

———. Letter to W. A. McCutchen. 8 Aug. 1901.

Spalding, Arthur W. *Captains of the Host.* Washington, D.C.: Review & Herald Publishing Assn., 1949.

———. *Origin and History of Seventh-day Adventists.* 4 vols. Washington, D.C.: Review & Herald Publishing Assn., 1962.

Spicer, W. A. "How the Spirit of Prophecy Met a Crisis." Berrien Springs, Mich. James White Library. Cited in Robert Haddock, "A History of the Doctrine of the Sanctuary in the Advent Movement" (B.D. thesis, Andrews University, 1970), pp. 335-36.

Steinweg, Bruno W. "Developments in the Teaching of Justification and Righteousness by Faith in the Seventh-day Adventist Church after 1900." Masters thesis, Seventh-day Adventist Theological Seminary, 1948.

Stibbs, A. M. *The Meaning of the Word 'Blood' in Scripture.* 3rd ed. London: Tyndale Press, 1962.

Strong, Augustus H. *Systematic Theology.* Old Tappan, N.J.: Fleming H. Revell Co., 1907.

Thomas, W. H. Griffith. *St. Paul's Epistle to the Romans.* Grand Rapids: Wm. B. Eerdmans Publishing Co., 1974.

Vande Vere, Emmett K. *The Wisdom Seekers.* Nashville: Southern Publishing Assn., 1972.

Venden, Morris L. *Salvation by Faith and Your Will.* Nashville: Southern Publishing Assn., 1979.

Waggoner, J. H. "Justification and Salvation." *Signs of the Times*, 30 Dec. 1886.

———. "Justification by Faith." *Signs of the Times*, 25 Nov. 1886.

———. *The Law of God: An Examination of the Testimony of Both Testaments.* Rochester, N.Y.: Advent Review Office, 1854.

———. "Note from Bro. Waggoner." *Review and Herald*, 18 July 1854, p. 188.

Walker, Jack D., ed. *Documents from the Palmdale Conference on Righteousness by Faith.* Goodlettsville, Tenn.: Jack D. Walker, 1976.

White, Ellen G. Diary (Christ Our Righteousness), 27 Feb. 1891. Manuscript 21, 1891, pp. 6-7.

———. "Camp-meeting at Williamsport, Pa." *Review and Herald*, 13 Aug. 1889, pp. 513-14.

———. *The Desire of Ages.* Mountain View, Calif.: Pacific Press Publishing Assn., 1898.

———. *Gospel Workers.* Revised and enlarged ed. Washington, D.C.: Review & Herald Publishing Assn., 1948.

———. *The Great Controversy.* Mountain View, Calif.: Pacific Press Publishing Assn., 1911.

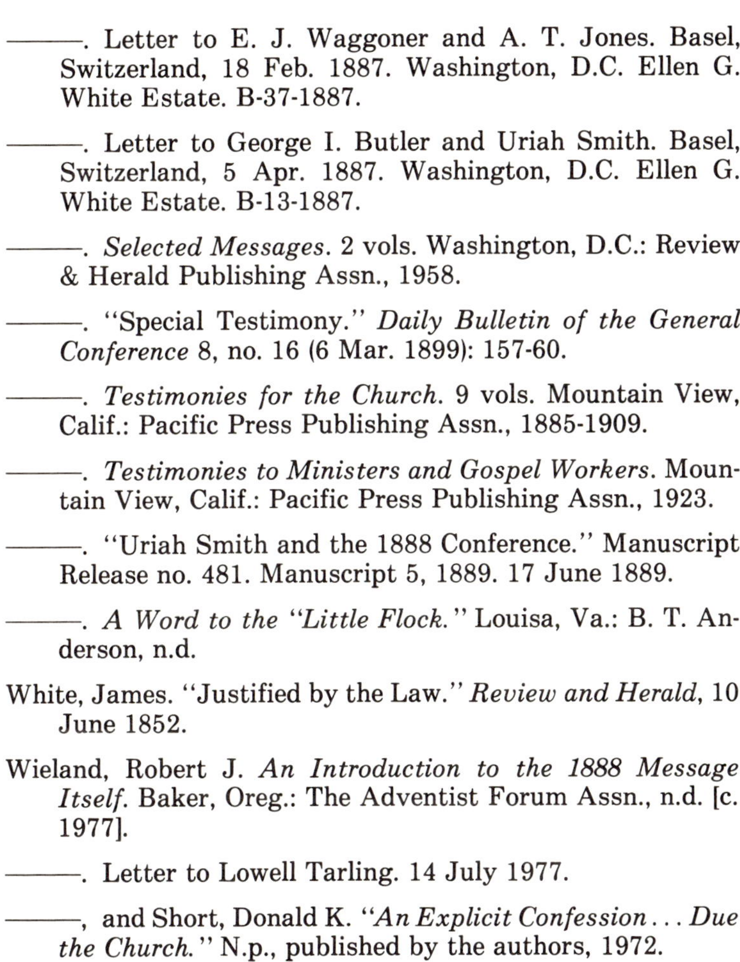

———. Letter to E. J. Waggoner and A. T. Jones. Basel, Switzerland, 18 Feb. 1887. Washington, D.C. Ellen G. White Estate. B-37-1887.

———. Letter to George I. Butler and Uriah Smith. Basel, Switzerland, 5 Apr. 1887. Washington, D.C. Ellen G. White Estate. B-13-1887.

———. *Selected Messages.* 2 vols. Washington, D.C.: Review & Herald Publishing Assn., 1958.

———. "Special Testimony." *Daily Bulletin of the General Conference* 8, no. 16 (6 Mar. 1899): 157-60.

———. *Testimonies for the Church.* 9 vols. Mountain View, Calif.: Pacific Press Publishing Assn., 1885-1909.

———. *Testimonies to Ministers and Gospel Workers.* Mountain View, Calif.: Pacific Press Publishing Assn., 1923.

———. "Uriah Smith and the 1888 Conference." Manuscript Release no. 481. Manuscript 5, 1889. 17 June 1889.

———. *A Word to the "Little Flock."* Louisa, Va.: B. T. Anderson, n.d.

White, James. "Justified by the Law." *Review and Herald,* 10 June 1852.

Wieland, Robert J. *An Introduction to the 1888 Message Itself.* Baker, Oreg.: The Adventist Forum Assn., n.d. [c. 1977].

———. Letter to Lowell Tarling. 14 July 1977.

———, and Short, Donald K. *"An Explicit Confession . . . Due the Church."* N.p., published by the authors, 1972.

———, and Short, Donald K. *1888 Re-examined.* In *A Warning and Its Reception,* edited by A. L. Hudson, Baker, Oreg.: Hudson Printing Co., n.d. [c. 1960].

Wood, Kenneth H. "Christmas 1976." *Review and Herald,* 23 Dec. 1976, p. 2.

———. "F. Y. I." [For Your Information]. Nos. 1-4. *Review and Herald,* 21 Oct. 1976, p. 2; 28 Oct. 1976, pp. 2, 19; 4 Nov. 1976, pp. 2, 15; 18 Nov. 1976, pp. 2, 13.

Waggoner Bibliography

Books and Pamphlets

Baptism: Its Significance. Bible Student's Library, no. 79. Oakland: Pacific Press Publishing Co., 1890.

Bible Studies on the Book of Romans. Baker, Oreg.: A. L. Hudson, n.d. A facsimile reproduction from the 1891 *General Conference Bulletin.*

Christ and His Righteousness. Oakland: Pacific Press Publishing Co., 1890. In 1972 a facsimile reproduction of the original edition was issued by Southern Publishing Association, Nashville, Tennessee.

A "Confession of Faith." N.p., n.d. The manuscript of this letter was the last thing written by Waggoner and was addressed to M. C. Wilcox. Found on Waggoner's desk after his sudden death, May 28, 1916, it was published posthumously at the request of friends.

The Cross of Christ. Apples of Gold Library, no. 15. Oakland: Pacific Press Publishing Co., 1894.

The Everlasting Covenant. London: International Tract Society, 1900.

Foreknowledge and Foreordination. Apples of Gold Library, no. 41. Oakland: Pacific Press Publishing Co., 1897.

The Full Assurance of Faith. Bible Student's Library, no. 64. Oakland: Pacific Press Publishing Co., 1890.

The Glad Tidings. London: International Tract Society, 1900. Within the last two years, the Judgment Hour Publishing Company, 309 Chevallum Rd., Palmwoods, Queensland, Australia, has republished this book in unedited and unrevised form.

The Glad Tidings. Edited and revised by Robert J. Wieland. Nashville: Southern Publishing Assn., 1972.

The Gospel in Creation. London: International Tract Society, 1893; Battle Creek, Mich.: Review & Herald Publishing House, 1894.

The Gospel in the Book of Galatians: A Review. Oakland: Pacific Press Publishing Co., 1888. A letter to George I. Butler, dated February 10, 1887. Republished by the Judgment Hour Publishing Co.

The Honor Due to God. Oakland: Pacific Press Publishing Co., 1884.

Letter and Spirit. Apples of Gold Library, no. 37. Oakland: Pacific Press Publishing Co., 1897.

Living by Faith: Christian Growth. Bible Student's Library, no. 75. Oakland: Pacific Press Publishing Co., 1890.

The Power of Forgiveness. Oakland: Pacific Press Publishing Co., 1890; London: International Tract Society, n.d.

Prophetic Lights: Some of the Prominent Prophecies of the Old and New Testaments, Interpreted by the Bible and History. Oakland: Pacific Press Publishing Co., 1889.

The Rest That Remains for the People of God. Bible Student's Library, no. 101. Oakland: Pacific Press Publishing Co., 1893.

Salvation in Jesus Christ. Apples of Gold Library, no. 64. Oakland: Pacific Press Publishing Co., 1899.

A Series of Readings Covering a Portion of the Ground Embraced in the Bible Course at Healdsburg College, 1883-1884. 1st and 2nd eds. 2 vols. Oakland: Pacific Press Publishing Co., n.d.

Sunday: The Origin of Its Observance in the Christian Church. Bible Student's Library, no. 80. Oakland: Pacific Press Publishing Co., n.d. [c. 1891].

The Sure Foundation and the Keys of the Kingdom. Bible Student's Library, no. 63. Oakland: Pacific Press Publishing Co., n.d.

Articles

Bible Echo and Signs of the Times (1886-1897)

"The Second Commandment." Oct. 1886, p. 154.

"Some Modern Criticisms." Nov. 1886, p. 162.

"Religion and Happiness." Nov. 1886, p. 170.

"Manner of Christ's Coming." June 1887, p. 90.

"Conditional Immortality—What Is It?" Nov. 1887, p. 170.

"One Probation Enough." Feb. 1888, p. 20.

"An Unwarranted Conclusion." May 1888, p. 66.

"Importance of Bible Study." June 1888, pp. 83-4.

"The Oracles of God." July 1888, p. 106.

"The Promise of His Coming." Nov. 1888, p. 170.

"Thine Is the Glory." Dec. 1888, pp. 185-86.

"Life and Death Opposite Terms." 1 Jan. 1889, p. 10.

"The Papacy." 15 Jan. 1889, pp. 25-6.

"The Papacy" (cont.). 1 Feb. 1889, p. 42.

"The Papacy" (cont.). 15 Feb. 1889, pp. 57-8.

"The Papacy" (cont.). 1 Mar. 1889, pp. 74-5.

"The Papacy" (concl.). 15 Mar. 1889, pp. 89-90.

"The First Dominion." 1 Apr. 1889, p. 105.

"The First Dominion" (concl.). 15 Apr. 1889, p. 122.

"The Call of Abraham." 1 May 1889, pp. 137-38.

"Baptized by Fire." 1 May 1889, p. 139.

"The Hope of the Promise." 15 May 1889, p. 154.

"The Rest That Remains." 3 June 1889, p. 170.

"The Rest That Remains" (concl.). 17 June 1889, p. 186.

"The Throne of David." 1 July 1889, pp. 201-2.

"The Throne of David" (cont.). 15 July 1889, p. 218.

"The Throne of David" (concl.). 1 Aug. 1889, pp. 233-34.

"Continue." 15 Aug. 1889, p. 250.

"The Divinity of Christ." 1 Sept. 1889, pp. 265-66.

"The Divinity of Christ" (cont.). 16 Sept. 1889, pp. 281-82.

"The Divinity of Christ" (cont.). 1 Oct. 1889, pp. 297-98.

"The Divinity of Christ" (cont.). 15 Oct. 1889, pp. 313-14.

"The Divinity of Christ" (concl.). 1 Nov. 1889, p. 330.

"Glorify God As God." 15 Nov. 1889, pp. 345-46.

"Principles and Precepts." 15 Jan. 1890, pp. 25-6.

"Is It a Sin?" 1 Feb. 1890, pp. 41-2.

"The Issues of the Present Time." 1 Mar. 1890, p. 74.

"Reasons against Sunday Laws." 15 Mar. 1890, p. 90.

"Why It Is." 1 May 1890, p. 138.

"The Reasonableness of Faith." 1 June 1890, p. 170.

"Real Forgiveness." 15 June 1890, p. 186.

"Saving Faith." 1 Aug. 1890, p. 233.

"How Righteousness Is Obtained." 1 Nov. 1890, p. 330.

"Principles and Precepts." 1 Dec. 1890, pp. 361-62.

"Christ Will Come." 15 Dec. 1890, p. 378.

"The Christian a Debtor." 15 June 1891, pp. 185-86.

"Exposition of 2 Cor. 3:7-11." 1 July 1891, pp. 201-2.

"Intellect Not Sufficient." 1 Aug. 1891, p. 233.

"Obedience in the Letter and Spirit." 1 Oct. 1891, p. 297.

"What the Gospel Teaches." 15 Oct. 1891, p. 313.

"From Faith to Faith." 15 Jan. 1892, pp. 26-7.

"Unprofitable Servants." 1 Feb. 1892, p. 41.

"Christ the End of the Law." 15 Feb. 1892, p. 57.

"Living by Faith." 15 Sept. 1892, p. 282.

"Christian Growth." 1 Oct. 1892, pp. 297-98.

"The Unconquerable Life." 15 Oct. 1892, pp. 313-14.

"Can We Keep the Sabbath?" 15 Nov. 1892, p. 345.

"Can We Keep the Sabbath?" (concl.). 1 Dec. 1892, pp. 361-62.

"Like As a Father." 15 Jan. 1893, pp. 26-7.

"Be of Good Courage." 1 Feb. 1893, p. 42.

"Baptism—Its Significance." 15 Feb. 1893, p. 58.

"Baptism—Its Significance" (concl.). 1 Mar. 1893, pp. 73-4.

"What Is the Gospel?" 1 May 1893, p. 138.

"The Work of the Gospel." 15 June 1893, p. 202.

"The Power Given to God's People." 1 July 1893, pp. 218-19.

"The Resurrection of Christ." 15 July 1893, pp. 234-35.

"The Power of the Resurrection." 1 Aug. 1893, p. 250.

"The Reign of Peace." 1 Sept. 1893, p. 282.

"Authoritative Statements of Evolution." 15 Sept. 1893, p. 298.

"Evolution and the Gospel." 1 Oct. 1893, pp. 313-14.

"Religious Boycotts." 15 Oct. 1893, p. 330.

"Christian Warfare." 15 Oct. 1893, p. 330.

"The Power of Forgiveness." 1 Nov. 1893, pp. 345-46.

"Recreation." 1 Nov. 1893, pp. 346-47.

"Move to Adjourn." 1 Dec. 1893, p. 378.

"Creative Power." 8 Dec. 1893, pp. 385-86.

"Cast Your Care on God." 19 Nov. 1894, pp. 354-55.

"What and Where Is Paradise?" 22 Apr. 1895, p. 122.

"Ethics of Sunday Legislation." 13 May 1895, p. 147.

"Working with Him." 26 Aug. 1895, p. 267.

"Parents and the State." 4 Nov. 1895, pp. 348-49.

"Hardening Pharaoh's Heart." 16 Dec. 1895, p. 387.

"Facts about the Sabbath." 23 Dec. 1895, pp. 394-95.

"Custom against Precept." 6 Jan. 1896, pp. 2-3.

"The Change of the Sabbath." 23 Mar. 1896, pp. 90-91.

"The Sin of Witchcraft." 6 Apr. 1896, pp. 105-6.

"The Wrong Man." 20 Apr. 1896, p. 114.

"Grace and Truth." 8 June 1896, p. 172.

"The 'Up-to-Date' Pulpit." 6 July 1896, p. 203.

"Intolerant of Evil." 13 July 1896, pp. 212-13.

"Not a Creed." 27 July 1896, p. 229.

"Spoken to You." 7 Sept. 1896, p. 276.

"Baptism." 12 Oct. 1896, pp. 315-16.

"The Only Successful Weapon against Error." 19 Oct. 1896, pp. 321-22.

"Understanding the Bible." 23 Nov. 1896, pp. 363-64.

"What Is Christmas?" 21 Dec. 1896, p. 394.

"The Nature of Christ's Kingdom." 4 Jan. 1897, p. 3.

"The Beast of Revelation 13 and 14." 26 Apr. 1897, pp. 129-32.

"God's Rest." 3 May 1897, pp. 137-39.

"A Negative Religion." 5 July 1897, pp. 210-11.

"Getting Rid of the Burden." 25 Oct. 1897, pp. 339-40.

"No Scripture Authority for Sunday Observance." 15 Nov. 1897, pp. 354-55.

"Power from on High." 6 Dec. 1897, p. 379.

"Imagining Difficulties." 13 Dec. 1897, p. 388.

General Conference Bulletin (1897, 1899, 1901)

"Studies in the Book of Hebrews." *General Conference Daily Bulletin* 1 (1897).

"Studies in Hebrews." *General Conference Bulletin* 2 (1897).

"Witnesses for God." *General Conference Bulletin* 2, no. 1 (First Quarter, 1897).

Daily Bulletin of the General Conference 8 (1899).

"The Water of Life." *Daily Bulletin of the General Conference* 8, no. 8 (24 Feb. 1899).

General Conference Bulletin 4 (1901). Bible studies and sermons.

Medical Missionary (1903-1905)

"Co-Workers with God." Apr. 1903, pp. 89-94.

"Co-Workers with God" (cont.). May 1903, pp. 120-21.

"Present Truth." July 1903, pp. 167-69.

"Present Truth" (cont.). Aug. 1903, pp. 196-98.

"Present Truth" (concl.). Sept. 1903, pp. 252-54.

"Healing through Faith, or Divine Healing." Nov. 1903, pp. 274-77.

"Healing through Faith" (cont.). Dec. 1903, pp. 300-302.

"Healing through Faith" (concl.). Jan. 1904, pp. 11-13.

"Daily Bread for Christian Workers." Devotional column. Apr. 1904, pp. 123-27.

"Daily Bread for Christian Workers." May 1904, pp. 160-64.

"Daily Bread for Christian Workers." June 1904, pp. 194-99.

"Daily Bread for Christian Workers." July 1904, pp. 212-216.

"The True Priesthood." Aug. 1904, pp. 243-45.

"Daily Bread for Christian Workers." Aug. 1904, pp. 260-64.

"Daily Bread for Christian Workers." Sept. 1904, pp. 283-87.

"Daily Bread for Christian Workers." Oct. 1904, pp. 326-31.

"The Philosophy of Healing." Nov. 1904, pp. 344-45.

"Daily Bread for Christian Workers." Nov. 1904, pp. 347-52.

"Daily Bread for Christian Workers." Dec. 1904, pp. 379-85.

"Saving, Not Stoning, Sinners." Jan. 1905, pp. 2-3.

"Eat Ye That Which Is Good." Feb. 1905, pp. 38-9.

"A Lesson for All Workers." Mar. 1905, pp. 67-9.

"New Light and New Sight." May 1905, pp. 130-31.

"Workers Together with God." June 1905, pp. 164-66.

"Preparation for Service." July 1905, pp. 213-14.

"Has God Arbitrarily Limited Man's Age?" Aug. 1905, pp. 242-43.

"An Incentive to Thoroughness." Sept. 1905, pp. 283-85.

"Is Any Afflicted? Let Him Pray." Oct. 1905, pp. 306-8.

"Our Father." Nov. 1905, pp. 338-39.

"The Holy Name." Dec. 1905, pp. 376-77.

Missionary Magazine (1902)

"Studies in the Gospel Message: The Hope of the Promise." Jan. 1902, pp. 14-17.

"Studies in the Gospel Message: A Vital Question Answered." Feb. 1902, pp. 60-63.

"Studies in the Gospel Message: The Law of the Spirit of Life." Apr. 1902, pp. 159-62.

Present Truth (1892-1900)

"What Is the Gospel?" 28 Jan. 1892, pp. 24-6.

"How Righteousness Is Obtained." 24 Mar. 1892, pp. 88-90.

"Prophecies Concerning the Messiah." 5 May 1892, p. 136.

"Prophecies Concerning the Messiah" (cont.). 2 June 1892, p. 168.

"Prophecies Concerning the Messiah" (cont.). 16 June 1892, p. 184.

"Prophecies Concerning the Messiah" (concl.). 30 June 1892, p. 200.

"Baptism—Its Significance." 14 July 1892, pp. 216-17.

"Life in Christ." 28 July 1892, p. 232.

"Good Works." 11 Aug. 1892, p. 248.

"The Miracles of Jesus." 25 Aug. 1892, pp. 264-65.

"The Inspired Word." 25 Aug. 1892, pp. 295-96.

"Righteousness and Life." 6 Oct. 1892, pp. 307-8.

"Saved by His Life." 6 Oct. 1892, p. 308.

"Being Justified." 20 Oct. 1892, pp. 323-24.

"Christ the Liberator." 17 Nov. 1892, p. 354.

"The Perfection of Wisdom." 17 Nov. 1892, pp. 355-56.

"The Power of the Resurrection." 29 Dec. 1892, pp. 402-3.

"Knowing the Truth." 29 Dec. 1892, p. 403.

"The Law and the Life." 26 Jan. 1893, pp. 19-20.

"The Commandments of God." 26 Jan. 1893, pp. 17-18.

"The Fulfilling of the Law." 26 Jan. 1893, pp. 18-19.

"A New Creation." 9 Feb. 1893, pp. 33-4.

"Promises." 9 Feb. 1893, pp. 34-6.

"In His Name." 23 Feb. 1893, pp. 49-50.

"The Growing Power in Plants." 23 Feb. 1893, p. 50.

"The Rest That Remains." 23 Feb. 1893, pp. 51-2.

"Justice and Mercy." 23 Feb. 1893, pp. 52-5.

"Justification by Works." 9 Mar. 1893, pp. 66-7.

"A Revival of Spiritualism." 23 Mar. 1893, pp. 83-7.

"Hear and Live." 6 Apr. 1893, pp. 100-101.

"The Power of the Resurrection." 4 May 1893, pp. 130-31.

"A Present Salvation." 18 May 1893, pp. 145-46.

"Saints." 1 June 1893, pp. 163-64.

"The Day of Jesus Christ." 15 June 1893, pp. 177-81.

"How to Get Knowledge." 6 July 1893, pp. 210-11.

"The Fruits of Righteousness." 13 July 1893, pp. 225-26.

"How Plants Grow." 13 July 1893, pp. 226-28.

"A Godly Life." 13 July 1893, pp. 228-29.

"The Love of God." 20 July 1893, pp. 241-42.

"The Suffering of Christ." 20 July 1893, pp. 242-44.

"The Lord's Day." 20 July 1893, pp. 244-45.

"The Sabbath and the Cross." 20 July 1893, pp. 245-47.

"Helping God." 3 Aug. 1893, pp. 273-74.

"Christ and Antichrist." 10 Aug. 1893, pp. 292-95.

"Christian Experience." 17 Aug. 1893, pp. 305-6.

"Why Did Christ Die?" 21 Sept. 1893, pp. 385-88.

"The Heavenly Sanctuary." 28 Sept. 1893, pp. 405-6.

"Mistaken Conceptions of Holiness." 12 Oct. 1893, pp. 435-36.

"Acquaintance with God." 19 Oct. 1893, pp. 450-51.

"A Wonderful Bargain." 26 Oct. 1893, pp. 467-68.

"The Eye of Faith." 2 Nov. 1893, pp. 483-84.

"Propitiation." 9 Nov. 1893, pp. 500-501.

"Heart Condemnation." 30 Nov. 1893, pp. 545-46.

"Dare You Trust Him?" 11 Jan. 1894, pp. 20-21.

"The Cross and Crosses." 22 Feb. 1894, pp. 115-17.

"Not a Creed." 22 Feb. 1894, p. 118.

"Confessing Christ in the Flesh." 8 Mar. 1894, pp. 149-53.

"A Lesson from Real Life." 31 May 1894, pp. 338-39.

"Studies in Romans: The Salutation." 21 June 1894, pp. 388-91.

"Studies in Romans: Debtor to All." 28 June 1894, pp. 402-5.

"Studies in Romans: The Righteousness of God." 5 July 1894, pp. 421-23.

"Studies in Romans: God's Revelation to Man." 12 July 1894, pp. 436-40.

"Studies in Romans: Universal Judgment." 19 July 1894, pp. 450-53.

"Studies in Romans: The Law and Judgment." 26 July 1894, pp. 466-68.

"Studies in Romans: Form and Fact." 2 Aug. 1894, pp. 482-84.

"Studies in Romans: Jew and Gentile." 9 Aug. 1894, pp. 498-500.

"Studies in Romans: The Sum of the Matter." 16 Aug. 1894, pp. 514-16.

"Studies in Romans: A Wonderful Manifestation." 23 Aug. 1894, pp. 530-32.

"Studies in Romans: The Justice of Mercy." 30 Aug. 1894, pp. 548-50.

"Studies in Romans: Establishing the Law." 6 Sept. 1894, pp. 562-64.

"Studies in Romans: The Blessing of Abraham." 13 Sept. 1894, pp. 508-82.

"Studies in Romans: Heir of the World." 20 Sept. 1894, pp. 595-97.

"Studies in Romans: The Surety of the Promise." 4 Oct. 1894, pp. 626-28.

"Studies in Romans: Saved by His Life." 11 Oct. 1894, pp. 642-45.

"Studies in Romans: The Free Gift." 18 Oct. 1894, pp. 658-60.

"Studies in Romans: Grace and Truth." 25 Oct. 1894, pp. 676-78.

"Studies in Romans: Crucified, Buried, and Raised." 1 Nov. 1894, pp. 690-92.

"Studies in Romans: Instruments of Righteousness." 8 Nov. 1894, pp. 706-8.

"Studies in Romans: Union with Christ." 15 Nov. 1894, pp. 722-24.

"Studies in Romans: The Law of Sin." 22 Nov. 1894, pp. 738-40.

"Studies in Romans: Freedom." 29 Nov. 1894, pp. 756-58.

"Studies in Romans: Sons of God." 6 Dec. 1894, pp. 770-72.

"Studies in Romans: Glorified Together." 13 Dec. 1894, pp. 786-88.

"Studies in Romans: Something Worth Knowing." 20 Dec. 1894, pp. 807-8.

"Studies in Romans: The Unspeakable Gift." 27 Dec. 1894, pp. 818-20.

"Studies in Romans: A Glorious Persuasion." 3 Jan. 1895, pp. 2-4.

"Studies in Romans: Who Are the Israelites?" 10 Jan. 1895, pp. 21-3.

"Studies in Romans: Accepted in the Beloved." 17 Jan. 1895, pp. 36-8.

"Studies in Romans: The Glorious Gospel." 31 Jan. 1895, pp. 66-8.

"Studies in Romans: All Israel Saved." 7 Feb. 1895, pp. 82-4.

"Studies in Romans: Some Practical Exhortations." 14 Feb. 1895, pp. 101-3.

"Studies in Romans: Christians and the State." 21 Mar. 1895, pp. 179-82.

"Studies in Romans: God the Only Judge." 4 July 1895, pp. 418-21.

"Studies in Romans: Living for Others." 11 July 1895, pp. 434-36.

"Studies in Romans: The Law of Christ." 25 July 1895, pp. 467-68.

"Studies in Romans: Confirming the Promises." 1 Aug. 1895, pp. 483-86.

"The Thing Spoken in the Word Itself." 9 Apr. 1896, p. 226.

"Letter and Spirit." 16 Apr. 1896, pp. 245-46.

"The All-Sufficient Life." 23 Apr. 1896, pp. 258-60.

"The Everlasting Gospel: The Gospel Message." 7 May 1896, pp. 292-95.

"The First Dominion: The Purchased Possession." 14 May 1896, pp. 305-8.

"The Call of Abraham: The Promise to Abraham." 21 May 1896, pp. 321-23.

"The Call of Abraham: Building an Altar." 28 May 1896, pp. 341-43.

"The Call of Abraham: Making a Covenant." 4 June 1896, pp. 355-56.

"Simply to Thy Cross I Cling." 11 June 1896, pp. 369-70.

"The Call of Abraham: The Flesh against the Spirit." 11 June 1896, pp. 371-72.

"The Judgment." 18 June 1896, pp. 383-85.

"The Call of Abraham: The Covenant Sealed." 18 June 1896, pp. 387-89.

"The Call of Abraham: The Covenant Sealed" (concl.). 25 June 1896, pp. 405-6.

"The Call of Abraham: The Test of Faith." 2 July 1896, pp. 421-23.

"The Call of Abraham: The Promise and the Oath." 9 July 1896, pp. 433-35.

"The Call of Abraham: The Call of Victory." 16 July 1896, pp. 451-52.

"The Promises to Israel: A General View." 23 July 1896, pp. 465-67.

"The Promises to Israel: Israel a Prince of God." 30 July 1896, pp. 483-86.

"The Promises to Israel: Israel in Egypt." 6 Aug. 1896, pp. 499-501.

"The Promises to Israel: The Time of the Promise." 13 Aug. 1896, pp. 517-18.

"Thine Is the Kingdom." 20 Aug. 1896, pp. 529-30.

"The Promises to Israel: The Reproach of Christ." 20 Aug. 1896, pp. 531-33.

"The Promises to Israel: Giving the Commission." 27 Aug. 1896, pp. 549-50.

"The Promises to Israel: Preaching the Gospel in Egypt." 3 Sept. 1896, pp. 563-64.

"The Power and the Glory." 10 Sept. 1896, pp. 577-78.

"Not a Creed." 10 Sept. 1896, p. 578.

"The Promises to Israel: How Pharaoh's Heart Was Hardened." 10 Sept. 1896, pp. 579-80.

"The Promises to Israel: Saved by the Life." 17 Sept. 1896, pp. 595-96.

"The Promises to Israel: The Final Deliverance." 24 Sept. 1896, pp. 611-13.

"The Promises to Israel: The Song of Deliverance." 1 Oct. 1896, pp. 627-28.

"The Promises to Israel: Bread from Heaven." 8 Oct. 1896, pp. 644-46.

"The Just Shall Live by Faith." 15 Oct. 1896, p. 658.

"The Promises to Israel: Life from God." 15 Oct. 1896, pp. 659-60.

"The Promises to Israel: Life from the Word." 22 Oct. 1896, pp. 675-76.

"His Saving Knowledge." 29 Oct. 1896, pp. 689-90.

"The Promises to Israel: Water from the Rock—Living Water." 29 Oct. 1896, pp. 692-94.

"The Promises to Israel: Object Teaching." 5 Nov. 1896, pp. 707-8.

"The Promises to Israel: The Entering of the Law." 12 Nov. 1896, pp. 723-25.

"The Promises to Israel: The Entering of the Law" (cont.). 19 Nov. 1896, pp. 739-41.

"The Promises to Israel: Sinai and Calvary." 26 Nov. 1896, pp. 756-57.

"The Promises to Israel: Mt. Sinai and Mt. Zion." 3 Dec. 1896, pp. 771-73.

"The Promises to Israel: The Covenants of Promise." 10 Dec. 1896, pp. 787-90.

"The Promises to Israel: The Veil and the Shadow." 17 Dec. 1896, pp. 805-7.

"The Promises to Israel: Two Laws." 24 Dec. 1896, pp. 819-21.

"The Promises to Israel: Entering the Promised Land." 31 Dec. 1896, pp. 835-37.

"The Promises to Israel: Vainglory and Defeat." 7 Jan. 1897, pp. 3-5.

"The Promises to Israel: Israel a Missionary People." 14 Jan. 1897, pp. 19-23.

"The Promises to Israel: The Promised Rest." 21 Jan. 1897, pp. 36-8.

"The Promises to Israel: The Promised Rest" (cont.). 28 Jan. 1897, pp. 51-3.

"The Promises to Israel: Another Day." 4 Feb. 1897, pp. 67-9.

"The Promises to Israel: Another Day" (cont.). 11 Feb. 1897, pp. 83-5.

"The Promises to Israel: Again in Captivity." 18 Feb. 1897, pp. 99-101.

"The Promises to Israel: Again in Captivity" (cont.). 25 Feb. 1897, pp. 115-17.

"The Promises to Israel: Again in Captivity" (concl.). 4 Mar. 1897, pp. 131-33.

"The Promises to Israel: The Time of the Promise at Hand." 11 Mar. 1897, pp. 147-49.

"The Promises to Israel: The Lost Tribes of Israel." 13 May 1897, pp. 291-92.

"The Gathering of Israel: The Everlasting Covenant Complete." 27 May 1897, pp. 321-26.

"He Hath Blinded Their Eyes." 10 June 1897, pp. 353-54.

"Imitators of God." 5 Jan. 1899, pp. 1-2.

"The Gospel of Isaiah: The Great Case at Law." 5 Jan. 1899, pp. 2-5.

"Studies in the Gospel of John: Revealing the Glory." 5 Jan. 1899, pp. 5-6.

"The Gospel of Isaiah: Regeneration or Destruction." 12 Jan. 1899, pp. 18-20.

"Studies in the Gospel of John: The New Birth." 12 Jan. 1899, pp. 20-22.

"The Gospel of Isaiah." 19 Jan. 1899, pp. 34-6.

"Studies in the Gospel of John: The Water of Life." 19 Jan. 1899, pp. 36-8.

"The Gospel of Isaiah: God Alone Is Great." 26 Jan. 1899, pp. 51-2.

"Studies in the Gospel of John: Healing the Nobleman's Son." 26 Jan. 1899, pp. 53-4.

"The Gospel of Isaiah: Saved and Sent." 2 Feb. 1899, pp. 66-8.

"Studies in the Gospel of John: Man's Rightful Authority." 2 Feb. 1899, pp. 68-70.

"Grace Abounding." 9 Feb. 1899, pp. 81-2.

"Studies in the Gospel of John: Christian Giving." 9 Feb. 1899, pp. 82-4.

"The Gospel of Isaiah: God Our Only Refuge and Strength." 9 Feb. 1899, pp. 85-7.

"The Gospel of the Spring: Seeds." 9 Feb. 1899, p. 90.

"Multiplying the Seed." 9 Feb. 1899, pp. 90-91.

"The Gospel of Isaiah: The Power and Glory of the Kingdom." 16 Feb. 1899, pp. 97-9.

"Studies in the Gospel of John: Living by the Father." 16 Feb. 1899, pp. 99-101.

"The Gospel of the Spring: Jesus, the True Seed." 16 Feb. 1899, p. 106.

"Studies from the Gospel of John: The Test of Truth." 23 Feb. 1899, pp. 114-15.

"The Gospel of Isaiah: Strength out of Weakness." 23 Feb. 1899, pp. 116-18.

"The Gospel of the Spring: Flowers." 23 Feb. 1899, p. 122.

"Spiritual Drink." 2 Mar. 1899, pp. 129-30.

"The Gospel of Isaiah: The Lord My Banner." 2 Mar. 1899, pp. 131-32.

"Studies from the Gospel of John: How Not to Believe." 2 Mar. 1899, pp. 133-34.

"The Gospel of the Spring: Bees." 2 Mar. 1899, pp. 138-39.

"Studies from the Gospel of John: The Good Shepherd." 9 Mar. 1899, pp. 146-47.

"The Gospel of Isaiah: The New Song." 9 Mar. 1899, pp. 148-50.

"The Gospel of the Spring: The Hope of Glory." 9 Mar. 1899, pp. 154-55.

"The Gospel of Isaiah: The Judgment upon Babylon." 16 Mar. 1899, pp. 163-64.

"Studies from the Gospel of John: Saved and Kept." 16 Mar. 1899, pp. 164-66.

"The Gospel of the Spring: Some Warning Lessons." 16 Mar. 1899, pp. 170-71.

"The Perfect Salvation." 23 Mar. 1899, pp. 177-79.

"The Gospel of Isaiah: Israel's Deliverance." 23 Mar. 1899, pp. 179-80.

"Studies from the Gospel of John: The Glory of God." 23 Mar. 1899, pp. 181-82.

"The Gospel of the Spring: The Birds." 23 Mar. 1899, p. 186.

"The Gospel of Isaiah: Selfish Ambition and Its Fall." 30 Mar. 1899, pp. 195-97.

"Studies from the Gospel of John: The Anointing at Bethany." 30 Mar. 1899, pp. 197-98.

"The Gospel of the Spring: The Work of the Holy Spirit." 30 Mar. 1899, p. 202.

"Studies from the Gospel of John: Jesus Teaching Humility." 6 Apr. 1899, pp. 210-13.

"The Gospel of Isaiah: The Devouring Curse." 6 Apr. 1899, pp. 214-15.

"The Gospel of the Spring: The Real Spring." 6 Apr. 1899, p. 218.

"The Gospel of Isaiah: Deliverance of God's People." 13 Apr. 1899, pp. 225-27.

"Studies from the Gospel of John: Words of Comfort." 13 Apr. 1899, pp. 228-31.

"The Gospel of the Spring: The Equinox." 13 Apr. 1899, pp. 234-35.

"Sowing to the Flesh." 20 Apr. 1899, pp. 241-42.

"Studies from the Gospel of John: The Comforter." 20 Apr. 1899, pp. 242-44.

"The Gospel of Isaiah: Trust and Protection." 20 Apr. 1899, pp. 244-46.

"Our Fellow Creatures." 20 Apr. 1899, p. 250.

"The Speaking Blood." 27 Apr. 1899, pp. 257-58.

"Studies from the Gospel of John: The Vine and the Branches." 27 Apr. 1899, pp. 258-60.

"The Gospel of Isaiah: God's Care for His People." 27 Apr. 1899, pp. 260-62.

"God's Messengers." 27 Apr. 1899, p. 266.

"The Wondrous Name." 4 May 1899, pp. 273-75.

"The Gospel of Isaiah: The Crown of Shame and the Crown of Glory." 4 May 1899, pp. 275-77.

"God's Temple and Its Glory." 11 May 1899, pp. 289-90.

"Studies from the Gospel of John: Denying the Lord." 11 May 1899, pp. 290-92.

"The Gospel of Isaiah: The Sure Foundation." 11 May 1899, pp. 292-94.

"Studies from the Gospel of John: The King before the Judgment Bar." 18 May 1899, pp. 305-7.

"The Gospel of Isaiah: The Righteous Judgment of God." 18 May 1899, pp. 307-9.

"Studies from the Gospel of John: A Finished Work." 25 May 1899, pp. 321-23.

"The Gospel of Isaiah: The Cause of Ignorance." 25 May 1899, pp. 324-26.

"Studies from the Gospel of John: Christ Risen." 1 June 1899, pp. 338-39.

"The Gospel of Isaiah: 'Too Deep for Jehovah.'" 1 June 1899, pp. 340-41.

"The Gospel of Isaiah: Worldly Alliance a Failure." 8 June 1899, pp. 357-59.

"The Gospel of Isaiah: Waiting to Be Gracious." 15 June 1899, pp. 371-74.

"The Gospel of Isaiah: The Reign of Righteousness." 22 June 1899, pp. 388-90.

"The Way of Holiness." 29 June 1899, pp. 401-2.

"The Gospel of Isaiah: Dwelling with Consuming Fire." 29 June 1899, pp. 405-7.

"The Gospel of Isaiah: 'The King in His Beauty.'" 6 July 1899, pp. 419-21.

"The Gospel of Isaiah: The Earth Desolated." 13 July 1899, pp. 436-37.

"The Gospel of Isaiah: The Earth Restored." 20 July 1899, pp. 452-53.

"The Gospel of Isaiah: A Prayer for Healing Answered." 27 July 1899, pp. 468-71.

"The Gospel of Isaiah: Hezekiah's Tribute of Thanksgiving." 3 Aug. 1899, pp. 483-85.

"The Gospel of Isaiah: Going to Babylon." 10 Aug. 1899, pp. 497-99.

"The Gospel of Isaiah: The Last Loud Gospel Cry." 17 Aug. 1899, pp. 516-18.

"The Gospel of Isaiah: The Comfort of the Gospel." 24 Aug. 1899, pp. 532-35.

"The Gospel of Isaiah: Preparing the Way of the Lord." 31 Aug. 1899, pp. 548-50.

"The Miracle of Harvest." 7 Sept. 1899, pp. 561-62.

"The Gospel of Isaiah: 'All Flesh Is Grass.'" 7 Sept. 1899, pp. 563-65.

"The Lord Shall Give That Which Is Good; and Our Land Shall Yield Her Increase." 14 Sept. 1899, pp. 577-78.

"The Gospel of Isaiah: 'The Lord God Will Come.'" 14 Sept. 1899, pp. 580-82.

"The Gospel of Isaiah: 'The Mighty God.'" 21 Sept. 1899, pp. 593-95.

"The Gospel of Isaiah: Strength for the Helpless." 28 Sept. 1899, pp. 609-11.

"Saved." 5 Oct. 1899, pp. 525-26.

"The Gospel of Isaiah: The Great Case in Court." 5 Oct. 1899, pp. 627-29.

"Our Dwelling Place." 12 Oct. 1899, pp. 641-43.

"The Gospel of Isaiah: The Summons to the Trial." 12 Oct. 1899, pp. 643-45.

"The Gospel of Isaiah: 'Fear Not!'" 19 Oct. 1899, pp. 659-61.

"The Gospel of Isaiah: The Lord's Servant." 26 Oct. 1899, pp. 675-77.

"The Gospel of Isaiah: A New Song." 2 Nov. 1899, pp. 691-93.

"The Gospel of Isaiah: Magnifying the Law." 9 Nov. 1899, pp. 708-10.

"The Gospel of Isaiah: 'I Am with Thee.'" 16 Nov. 1899, pp. 721-24.

"The Blood of Sprinkling." 23 Nov. 1899, pp. 737-38.

"The Gospel of Isaiah: God's Witnesses." 23 Nov. 1899, pp. 738-40.

"I Am the Bread of Life." 30 Nov. 1899, pp. 753-55.

"The Gospel of Isaiah: The Sin-Bearer." 30 Nov. 1899, pp. 755-58.

"The Gospel of Isaiah: The Gift of the Spirit." 7 Dec. 1899, pp. 773-75.

"The Gospel of Isaiah: A Stupid, False Witness." 14 Dec. 1899, pp. 788-90.

"The Gospel of Isaiah: Abolishing the Enmity." 21 Dec. 1899, pp. 804-6.

"The Fall of Babylon: God, the Ruler of Nations." 28 Dec. 1899, pp. 819-21.

"The Gospel of Isaiah: The Unseen God." 4 Jan. 1900, pp. 1-3.

"The Gospel of Isaiah: Object of the Earth's Creation." 11 Jan. 1900, pp. 20-22.

"Fulfilling All Righteousness." 18 Jan. 1900, pp. 33-5.

"The Gospel of Isaiah: The God That Can Save." 18 Jan. 1900, pp. 35-8.

"The Gospel of Isaiah: The Downfall of Pride." 25 Jan. 1900, pp. 51-2.

"The Gospel of Isaiah: The Peace of Righteousness." 1 Feb. 1900, pp. 65-7.

"The Gospel of Isaiah: The Despised One Chosen." 8 Feb. 1900, pp. 84-6.

"Healthful Hints: The Gospel of Life." 8 Feb. 1900, pp. 93-4.

"The Gospel of Isaiah: The Earth's Interest in Redemption." 15 Feb. 1900, pp. 97-9.

"Temperance: Health by Faith." 15 Feb. 1900, pp. 109-10.

"The Gospel of Isaiah: The Triumph of Submission." 22 Feb. 1900, pp. 116-18.

"Temperance: Receiving the Life That Is Manifested." 22 Feb. 1900, pp. 125-26.

"The Gospel of Isaiah: Everlasting Righteousness Our Salvation." 1 Mar. 1900, pp. 131-33.

"The Gospel of Isaiah: The Power That Saves." 8 Mar. 1900, pp. 145-47.

"Temperance: The Proper Diet for Man." 8 Mar. 1900, pp. 157-58.

"The Gospel of Isaiah: Beautiful Preachers of a Glorious Message." 15 Mar. 1900, pp. 161-63.

"Temperance: Food Substitutes." 15 Mar. 1900, pp. 173-74.

"The Gospel of Isaiah: The Arm of the Lord." 22 Mar. 1900, pp. 180-82.

"The Gospel of Isaiah: The Silent Sufferer." 29 Mar. 1900, pp. 195-97.

"The Gospel of Isaiah: The Building Up of Jerusalem." 5 Apr. 1900, pp. 209-11.

"The Gospel of Isaiah: A Gracious Offer to the Poor." 12 Apr. 1900, pp. 225-27.

"The Gospel of Isaiah: Israel, the Gentiles, and the Sabbath." 19 Apr. 1900, pp. 241-43.

"The Gospel of Isaiah: Dwellers on High." 26 Apr. 1900, pp. 257-59.

"The Gospel of Isaiah: A Delightful Day." 3 May 1900, pp. 273-76.

"The Gospel of Isaiah: A Terrible Indictment against the Church." 10 May 1900, pp. 291-93.

"The Gospel of Isaiah: The Restoration of Zion." 17 May 1900, pp. 307-9.

"The Gospel of Isaiah: The Clothing Which God Gives." 24 May 1900, pp. 321-24.

"The Gospel of Isaiah: God's Watchfulness and Solicitude for His People." 31 May 1900, pp. 340-41.

"The Gospel of Isaiah: The Mighty Saviour." 7 June 1900, pp. 353-55.

"The Gospel of Isaiah: The Revelation of God." 14 June 1900, pp. 371-72.

"I AM." 21 June 1900, pp. 385-87.

"The Gospel of Isaiah: The Glorious Inheritance." 21 June 1900, pp. 387-89.

"The Practical Application of Justification by Faith in Everyday Life." 26 July 1900, pp. 467-70.

"Living by Faith." 2 Aug. 1900, pp. 484-86.

Review and Herald (1902-1903)

"Health by Faith." 21 Jan. 1902, p. 37

"The Gospel of Life." 11 Feb. 1902, p. 85.

"Why Do We Eat?" 25 Mar. 1902, p. 181.

"The Work of the Holy Spirit." 8 Apr. 1902, p. 9.

"The Message of the Spring." 22 Apr. 1902, p. 9.

"The Last Appeal." 27 May 1902, p. 11.

"The Blotting Out of Sin." 30 Sept. 1902, p. 8.

"A Confidential Word with a Penitent Soul." 14 Oct. 1902, p. 8.

"The Model Religious Life." 30 Dec. 1902, p. 11.

"The Manger and the Cross." 6 Jan. 1903, p. 9.

"A Whole Man." 31 Mar. 1903, p. 13.

"The Labor Problem." 21 Apr. 1903, p. 9.

"Sabbath-Keeping." 12 May 1903, p. 10.

"The Spirit of Prophecy." 23 June 1903, p. 9.

Signs of the Times (1884-1899)

"Worshiping in Letter and Spirit." 12 June 1884, pp. 360-61.

"An Important Question." 19 June 1884, pp. 377-78.

"Nature of the Law." 26 June 1884, p. 392.

"Condemned and Justified." 3 July 1884, pp. 408-9.

"A New Creature in Christ." 17 July 1884, pp. 424-25.

"Object of Christ's Coming." 24 July 1884, p. 441.

"Christ the End of the Law." 24 July 1884, p. 442.

"Christ the End of the Law" (concl.). 7 Aug. 1884, pp. 473-74.

"Under the Law." 28 Aug. 1884, p. 520.

"Under the Law" (cont.). 4 Sept. 1884, p. 537.

"Under the Law" (cont.). 11 Sept. 1884, pp. 553-54.

"Under the Law" (concl.). 18 Sept. 1884, pp. 569-70.

"What Constitutes a Christian?" 23 Oct. 1884, pp. 633-34.

"The Mission of Christ." 30 Oct. 1884, pp. 649-50.

"The Salvation Army." 4 Dec. 1884, pp. 728-29.

"Mercy and Justice." 26 Feb. 1885, pp. 137-38.

"The Sure Foundation." 8 Oct. 1885, pp. 601-2.

"'From Adam to Moses.'" 29 Oct. 1885, p. 649.

"Which Is Evangelical?" 12 Nov. 1885, p. 681.

"Judged by the Law." 26 Nov. 1885, pp. 712-13.

"Principles and Precepts." 17 Dec. 1885, pp. 760-61.

"The Law of God—For Whom Made." 24 Dec. 1885, p. 777.

"What the Gospel Teaches." 7 Jan. 1886, pp. 6-7.

"The Law and the Gospel Co-extensive." 14 Jan. 1886, pp. 23-4.

"Nature of the Law." 21 Jan. 1886, pp. 39-40.

"Nature of the Law" (concl.). 28 Jan. 1886, p. 55.

"Jurisdiction of the Law." 4 Feb. 1886, pp. 71-2.

"Jurisdiction of the Law" (cont.). 11 Feb. 1886, p. 87.

"Jurisdiction of the Law" (cont.). 18 Feb. 1886, pp. 103-4.

"Jurisdiction of the Law" (concl.). 25 Feb. 1886, p. 119.

"Perpetuity of the Law." 4 Mar. 1886, pp. 134-35.

"The Foundation of God's Government." 11 Mar. 1886, pp. 151-52.

"Doers of the Law." 18 Mar. 1886, p. 167.

"Justified by Faith." 25 Mar. 1886, pp. 183-84.

"Justification and Sanctification." 1 Apr. 1886, pp. 199-200.

"Christ the End of the Law." 8 Apr. 1886, pp. 215-16.

"Abolishing the Enmity." 15 Apr. 1886, pp. 231-32.

"The Handwriting of Ordinances." 22 Apr. 1886, pp. 247-48.

"Under the Law." 6 May 1886, pp. 263-64.

"Under the Law" (cont.). 13 May 1886, pp. 278-79.

"Under the Law" (cont.). 27 May 1886, p. 310.

"Under the Law" (concl.). 3 June 1886, pp. 326-27.

"Brief Comments on Romans 7." 17 June 1886, pp. 359-60.

"Brief Comments on Romans 7" (concl.). 24 June 1886, p. 374.

"Practical Thoughts on Psalm 63." 1 July 1886, pp. 390-91.

"Comments on Galatians 3." No. 1. 8 July 1886, p. 406.

"Comments on Galatians 3." No. 2. 15 July 1886, pp. 422-23.

"Comments on Galatians 3." No. 3. 22 July 1886, p. 438.

"Comments on Galatians 3." No. 4. 29 July 1886, p. 454.

"Comments on Galatians 3." No. 5. 5 Aug. 1886, p. 470.

"Comments on Galatians 3." No. 6. 12 Aug. 1886, p. 486.

"Comments on Galatians 3." No. 7. 19 Aug. 1886, p. 502.

"Comments on Galatians 3." No. 8. 26 Aug. 1886, pp. 518-19.

"Comments on Galatians 3." No. 9. 2 Sept. 1886, pp. 534-35.

"In the Law." 16 Sept. 1886, p. 566.

"Things We Should Know." No. 1. 27 Jan. 1887, p. 54.

"The Curse of the Law." 3 Feb. 1887, pp. 70-71.

"Things We Should Know." No. 2. 10 Feb. 1887, p. 86.

"Creation and Redemption." 31 Mar. 1887, pp. 199-200.

"Faith and Humility." 2 June 1887, p. 326.

"Blessed Are They That Do." 9 June 1887, p. 342.

"Born of God." 16 June 1887, pp. 358-59.

"Faith and Works." 23 June 1887, p. 376.

"What Condemns Men." 30 June 1887, pp. 390-91.

"Different Kinds of Righteousness." 24 Feb. 1888, p. 119.

"Fulfilling the Law." 13 Apr. 1888, p. 230.

"Lawful Use of the Law." 13 July 1888, p. 422.

"Forgiveness Real, Not Pretended." 3 Aug. 1888, p. 470.

"Luther on the Use of the Law." 7 Sept. 1888, pp. 547-48.

"Luther on the Use of the Law" (concl.). 14 Sept. 1888, pp. 563-64.

"Editorial Correspondence." 2 Nov. 1888, p. 662.

"A Servant of Jesus Christ." 7 Jan. 1889, pp. 6-7.

"The Gospel of God." 14 Jan. 1889, pp. 22-3.

"God Manifest in the Flesh." 21 Jan. 1889, pp. 38-9.

"The Power of Christ." 28 Jan. 1889, pp. 54-5.

"The Obedience of Faith." 4 Feb. 1889, p. 71.

"Saints of God." 11 Feb. 1889, pp. 86-7.

"The Church in Rome." 18 Feb. 1889, pp. 102-3.

"Established by Spiritual Gifts." 25 Feb. 1889, pp. 118-19.

"The Christian a Debtor." 4 Mar. 1889, p. 134.

"The Gospel the Power of God." 11 Mar. 1889, pp. 150-51.

"The Law in the Gospel." 18 Mar. 1889, pp. 166-67.

"The Divinity of Christ." 25 Mar. 1889, p. 182.

"Living by Faith." 25 Mar. 1889, pp. 182-83.

"Faith and Humility." 1 Apr. 1889, p. 198.

"The Divinity of Christ" (cont.). 1 Apr. 1889, p. 198.

"'From Faith to Faith.'" 1 Apr. 1889, p. 199.

"Holding the Truth in Unrighteousness." 8 Apr. 1889, p. 214.

"The Divinity of Christ" (cont.). 8 Apr. 1889, p. 214.

"Without Excuse." 22 Apr. 1889, p. 246.

"The Divinity of Christ" (cont.). 22 Apr. 1889, pp. 246-47.

"Divinity of Christ" (concl.). 6 May 1889, p. 262.

"Glorify God As God." 13 May 1889, p. 278.

"What It Is to Know God." 20 May 1889, pp. 294-95.

"Cause and Result of Unthankfulness." 1 July 1889, p. 390.

"Vain in Their Imaginations." 8 July 1889, p. 406.

"Exposition of 2 Cor. 3:7-11." 5 Aug. 1889, pp. 471-72.

"Exposition of 2 Cor. 3:7-11" (concl.). 12 Aug. 1889, p. 486.

"Faith and Humility." 19 Aug. 1889, p. 502.

"Nature of Christ." 21 Oct. 1889, pp. 631-32.

"Obedience Past and Present." 3 Feb. 1890, p. 70.

"Christ, the Sinless One." 9 June 1890, p. 342.

"Unrighteous Judgment, Self-Condemnation." 16 June 1890, pp. 358-59.

"Goodness Leading to Repentance." 23 June 1890, pp. 374-75.

"According to His Deeds." 30 June 1890, p. 390.

"The Righteousness Which Is in the Law." 30 June 1890, p. 391.

"The Advantage of the Jew." 14 July 1890, pp. 410-11.

"Sinning without Law." 21 July 1890, pp. 417-18.

"The True Circumcision." 28 July 1890, pp. 426-27.

"Romans 3:9-12." 11 Aug. 1890, pp. 442-43.

"Romans 3:9-12" (concl.). 25 Aug. 1890, pp. 457-58.

"No Justification by the Law." 1 Sept. 1890, pp. 466-67.

"How Righteousness Is Obtained." 8 Sept. 1890, pp. 473-74.

"Not a Debt, but a Gift." 22 Sept. 1890, pp. 489-90.

"The Blessing of Abraham." 29 Sept. 1890, pp. 497-98.

"For Our Sake Also." 12 Oct. 1890, pp. 513-14.

"Principles and Precepts." 20 Oct. 1890, pp. 521-22.

"Peace with God." 26 Jan. 1891, pp. 25-6.

"Patience, Its Development and Fruit." 16 Feb. 1891, pp. 49-50.

"Life from the Word." 21 Nov. 1892, pp. 36-7.

"Acceptance with God." 26 Dec. 1892, pp. 118-19.

"The Unconquerable Life." 27 Mar. 1893, p. 323.

"The Power of Forgiveness." 10 Apr. 1893, pp. 355-56.

"The Life of the Word." 17 Apr. 1893, p. 371.

"Being Justified." 1 May 1893, p. 403.

"The Power of the Name." 8 May 1893, pp. 419-20.

"Christ the Bread of Life." 29 May 1893, p. 453.

"Christ the Life Giver." 5 June 1893, p. 471.

"Obstacles to the Gospel." 21 Aug. 1893, pp. 647-48.

"The Object of the Sabbath." 11 Sept. 1893, p. 693.

"True Sabbath Keeping." 25 Sept. 1893, p. 725.

"The Reign of Peace." 9 Oct. 1893, pp. 757-58.

"A Lesson for All Time." 4 July 1895, pp. 401-3.

"God's Glory His Gospel." 25 July 1895, p. 449.

"Saved by His Life." 1 Aug. 1895, pp. 465-66.

"Judaism and Christianity." 1 Aug. 1895, pp. 466-67.

"The Waves and the Rock." 15 Aug. 1895, pp. 497-98.

"Justified by Works." 15 Aug. 1895, pp. 498-99.

"Perfect yet Growth." 29 Aug. 1895, p. 531.

"Carrying the Light." 5 Sept. 1895, pp. 546-47.

"On Trial." 12 Sept. 1895, pp. 561-64.

"They Cannot Be Separated." 19 Sept. 1895, pp. 577-78.

"'Another Day'—'To-Day.'" 19 Sept. 1895, pp. 578-79.

"The Spirit and the Word." 3 Oct. 1895, p. 609.

"Everything from Heaven." 3 Oct. 1895, pp. 609-10.

"Studies in Romans." 17 Oct. 1895, pp. 642-44.

"Studies in Romans: Debtor to All." 24 Oct. 1895, pp. 658-60.

"Mystery of Godliness." 31 Oct. 1895, p. 688.

"The Great Gift." 7 Nov. 1895, pp. 689-90.

"Studies in Romans: The Righteousness of God." 7 Nov. 1895, pp. 690-92.

"Studies in Romans: God's Revelation to Man." 14 Nov. 1895, pp. 706-9.

"Studies in Romans: Universal Judgment." 21 Nov. 1895, pp. 722-25.

"Studies in Romans: The Law and Judgment." 5 Dec. 1895, pp. 755-57.

"Studies in Romans: Form and Fact." 12 Dec. 1895, pp. 771-73.

"Studies in Romans: Jew and Gentile." 2 Jan. 1896, pp. 2-4.

"Studies in Romans: The Sum of the Matter." 9 Jan. 1896, pp. 18-20.

"Studies in Romans: A Wonderful Manifestation." 16 Jan. 1896, pp. 35-6.

"Studies in Romans: The Justice of Mercy." 23 Jan. 1896, pp. 51-2.

"Studies in Romans: Establishing the Law." 6 Feb. 1896, pp. 82-3.

"Studies in Romans: The Blessing of Abraham." 13 Feb. 1896, pp. 98-100.

"Studies in Romans: 'Heir of the World.'" 20 Feb. 1896, pp. 115-16.

"Studies in Romans: The Surety of the Promise." 27 Feb. 1896, pp. 130-31.

"Studies in Romans: 'Saved by His Life.'" 5 Mar. 1896, pp. 146-48.

"Studies in Romans: The Free Gift." 12 Mar. 1896, pp. 163-65.

"Studies in Romans: Grace and Truth." 26 Mar. 1896, pp. 194-96.

"Studies in Romans: Crucified, Buried, and Raised." 2 Apr. 1896, pp. 210-11.

"Studies in Romans: Instruments of Righteousness." 9 Apr. 1896, pp. 228-29.

"Studies in Romans: Union with Christ." 16 Apr. 1896, pp. 243-44.

"Studies in Romans: The Law of Sin." 23 Apr. 1896, pp. 259-60.

"Studies in Romans: Freedom." 30 Apr. 1896, pp. 275-76.

"Studies in Romans: Sons of God." 14 May 1896, pp. 306-7.

"Studies in Romans: Glorified Together." 21 May 1896, pp. 322-23.

"Studies in Romans: Something Worth Knowing." 28 May 1896, pp. 338-39.

"Studies in Romans: The Unspeakable Gift." 11 June 1896, pp. 354-56.

"Studies in Romans: A Glorious Persuasion." 18 June 1896, pp. 370-71.

"The All-Sufficient Life." 25 June 1896, pp. 391-92.

"Studies in Romans: Who Are Israelites?" 9 July 1896, pp. 418-19.

"Studies in Romans: Accepted in the Beloved." 16 July 1896, pp. 434-35.

"Studies in Romans: The Glorious Gospel." 23 July 1896, pp. 450-53.

"Studies in Romans: All Israel Saved." 30 July 1896, pp. 466-68.

"Studies in Romans: Some Practical Exhortations." 6 Aug. 1896, pp. 483-84.

"Studies in Romans: Christians and the State." 13 Aug. 1896, pp. 489-90.

"Studies in Romans: God the Only Judge." 20 Aug. 1896, pp. 514-16.

"Studies in Romans: Living for Others." 27 Aug. 1896, pp. 531-32.

"Studies in Romans: The Law of Christ." 3 Sept. 1896, pp. 546-47.

"Studies in Romans: Confirming the Promises." 10 Sept. 1896, pp. 562-64.

"Enforcing the Law of God." 7 Jan. 1897, pp. 2-3.

"Letter and Spirit." 14 Jan. 1897, pp. 18-19.

"The Greatness of His Gentleness." 21 Jan. 1897, p. 35.

"The Nature of God's Commandment." 28 Jan. 1897, pp. 50-51.

"The Will of God." 25 Feb. 1897, p. 115.

"The True Israel." 4 Mar. 1897, p. 130.

"Boldness to Enter In." 25 Mar. 1897, pp. 178-79.

"The Knowledge of Want." 1 Apr. 1897, p. 195.

"Speculation and Faith." 8 Apr. 1897, p. 211.

"The Everlasting Kingdom." 27 May 1897, pp. 322-23.

"Thine Is the Kingdom." 1 July 1897, pp. 385-86.

"The Power and the Glory." 8 July 1897, pp. 401-2.

"Christ As Teacher." 15 July 1897, p. 417.

"Himself He Can Not Save." 22 July 1897, pp. 433-34.

"The Wisdom of Jesus." 12 Aug. 1897, pp. 481-82.

"Independence." 26 Aug. 1897, pp. 513-14.

"A Lesson in Ruling." 2 Sept. 1897, p. 529.

"The Light of the World." 9 Sept. 1897, pp. 545-46.

"The Great Sacrifice." 30 Sept. 1897, pp. 593-94.

"His Saving Knowledge." 14 Oct. 1897, pp. 626-27.

"How to Love God." 28 Oct. 1897, pp. 658-59.

"Acceptance with God." 4 Nov. 1897, pp. 673-74.

"Greater Works Than These." 9 Dec. 1897, p. 754.

"Galatians 1:1-5." 24 Nov. 1898, pp. 738-40.

"Galatians 1:6-10: There Is Only One Gospel." 1 Dec. 1898, pp. 755-56.

"Galatians 1:13-24: A Zealous Persecutor Arrested." 8 Dec. 1898, pp. 770-72.

"Galatians 2:1-10: The Truth of the Gospel." 15 Dec. 1898, pp. 787-88.

"Galatians 2:6-16: Justified by the Faith of Christ." 22 Dec. 1898, pp. 803-5.

Galatians 2:17-21; 3:1: The Ever-Present Cross." 18 Jan. 1899, pp. 51-3.

"Galatians 3:1-10: The Blessing and the Curse." 25 Jan. 1899, pp. 67-9.

"Galatians 3:10-14: Redeemed from the Curse." 1 Feb. 1899, pp. 83-5.

"Galatians 3:15-18: The Promise and Its Surety." 8 Feb. 1899, pp. 99-100.

"Galatians 3:15-22: The Promise and the Law." 15 Feb. 1899, pp. 115-16.

"Galatians 3:22-29: From Prison to a Palace." 22 Feb. 1899, pp. 131-32.

"Galatians 4:1-7: The Adoption of Sons." 8 Mar. 1899, pp. 163-64.

"Galatians 4:7-31; 5:1: Bond-Servants and Freemen." 15 Mar. 1899, pp. 180-81.

"Galatians 4:7-31; 5:1: Bond-Servants and Freemen" (concl.). 22 Mar. 1899, p. 196.

"Galatians 5:1: Christ-Given Freedom." 5 Apr. 1899, p. 228.

"Galatians 5:1-13: Faith Which Works by Love." 12 Apr. 1899, pp. 244-45.

"Galatians 5:13-15: Love the Fulfilling of the Law." 19 Apr. 1899, pp. 260-61.

"Galatians 5:16-26: The Flesh, the Spirit, and the Law." 26 Apr. 1899, pp. 276-77.

"Galatians 6:1-3: The Law of Christ." 3 May 1899, pp. 292-93.

"Galatians 6:1-10: Improving the Opportunity." 10 May 1899, p. 308.

"Galatians 6:12-18: The Glory of the Cross." 17 May 1899, pp. 324-25.